C000193844

SUBJECTS OF ANALYSIS

THOMAS OGDEN is a graduate of the Yale School of Medicine and the San Francisco Psychoanalytic Institute. Dr Ogden is a full member of the International Psychoanalytic Association. He has served as an Associate Psychiatrist at the Tavistock Clinic, London, and is currently Co-director of the Center for the Advanced Study of the Psychoses, a member of the faculty of the San Francisco Psychoanalytic Institute, and a Supervising and Training Analyst at the Psychoanalytic Institute of Northern California. Dr Ogden is the author of *The Primitive Edge of Experience, The Matrix of the Mind: Object Relations and the Psychoanalytic Dialogue*, and *Projective Identification and Psychotherapeutic Technique*. He teaches, supervises, and maintains a private practice of psychoanalysis in San Francisco.

SUBJECTS OF ANALYSIS

Thomas H. Ogden

London

KARNAC BOOKS

Certain chapters in this book are based on prior publications of the author who gratefully acknowledges permission from the following journals to reprint this previously published material.

Chapter 2: "The Dialectically Constituted/Decentred Subject of Psychoanalysis. I. The Freudian Subject", *International Journal of Psycho-Analysis, 73*:517–526, 1992 (Copyright © Institute of Psycho-Analysis); Chapters 3 and 4: "The Dialectically Constituted/Decentred Subject of Psychoanalysis. II. The Contributions of Klein and Winnicott", *International Journal of Psycho-Analysis, 73*:613–626, 1992 (Copyright © Institute of Psycho-Analysis); Chapter 5: "The Analytic Third: Working with Intersubjective Clinical Facts", *International Journal of Psycho-Analysis, 75*:3–20, 1994 (Copyright © Institute of Psycho-Analysis); Chapter 7: "The Concept of Interpretive Action", *Psychoanalytic Quarterly, 63* (2), 1994 (Copyright © The Psychoanalytic Quarterly, Inc.); Chapter 8: "Analysing the Matrix of Transference", *International Journal of Psycho-Analysis, 72*:593–605, 1991 (Copyright © Institute of Psycho-Analysis); Chapter 9: "Some Theoretical Comments on Personal Isolation", *Psychoanalytic Dialogues, 1*:377–390, 1991 (Copyright © The Analytic Press); Chapter 10: "An Interview with Thomas Ogden", *Psychoanalytic Dialogues, 1*:361–376, 1991 (Copyright © The Analytic Press).

First published in 1994 by
H. Karnac (Books) Ltd.
58 Gloucester Road
London SW7 4QY

By arrangement with Jason Aronson, Inc.

British Library Cataloguing in Publication Data

A CIP catalogue record for this book is available from the British Library.

ISBN: 1 85575 101 1

Printed in Great Britain by BPC Wheatons Ltd, Exeter

For L. Bryce Boyer,
with love and gratitude,
for teaching me what it means to be a
psychoanalyst

The first sentence of every novel should be:
"Trust me, this will take time but there is order here,
very faint, very human." Meander if you want to get
to town.
Michael Ondaatje, *In the Skin of a Lion,* 1987

Contents

1

On Becoming a Subject

It is too late to turn back. Having read the opening words of this book you have already begun to enter into the unsettling experience of finding yourself becoming a subject whom you have not yet met, but nonetheless recognize. The reader of this book must create a voice with which to speak (think) the words (thoughts) comprising it. Reading is not simply a matter of considering, weighing, or even of trying out the ideas and experiences that are presented by the writer. Reading involves a far more intimate form of encounter. You, the reader, must allow me to occupy you, your thoughts, your mind, since I have no voice with which to speak other than yours. If you are to read this book, you must allow yourself to think my thoughts while I must allow myself to become your thoughts and in that moment neither of us will be able to lay claim to the thought as our own exclusive creation.

The conjunction of my words and your mental voice does not represent a form of ventriloquism. A more complex and interesting human event is involved. A third subject is created in the experience of reading that is not reducible to either writer or reader. The creation of a third subject (that exists in tension with the writer and the reader as separate subjects) is the essence of the experience of reading, and, as will be explored in this volume, is also at the core of the psychoanalytic experience.

In writing these sentences, I choose each word and phrase and speak to myself through the voice of the reader whom I have created in my own mind. It is the otherness of the reader (whom I imagine and anticipate in my own internal division of myself into writer and reader, subject and object) that allows me to hear myself in preparation for your reading. In your reading, you generate a voice from my words that will create me in a broader sense than I am able to create myself. In that process you and I shall have created one another as a subject who has not existed to this point.

The reader and writer do not create one another ahistorically. The present in which the third subject comes into being is not simply the current moment, but "the present moment of the past" (Eliot 1919), which (past) speaks through us as much as we speak through one another. Laius's, and later, Oedipus's attempts to create an ahistorical present set in motion the cascade of events leading to the deafening roar of the insistence of history and of mortality. We must recognize ourselves in Laius's and Oedipus's efforts to escape history, since each of us resists experiencing ourselves as spoken as well as speaking. Art, literature, history, philosophy, and psychoanalysis all teach us, despite our protestations, that we are indeed spoken, not only by the historical Other, but by the unconscious Other and the intersubjective Other.

You, the reader, will oppose me, deny me, perhaps humor me, but never entirely give way to me. This book will not be "understood" by you; you will not simply receive it, incorporate it, digest it, or the like. To the degree that you will have anything at all to do with it, you will transform it. (The word *transform* is too tepid a word to describe what you will do to it.) You will destroy it, and out of that destruction (in that destruction) will come a sound that you will not fully recognize. The sound will be a voice, but it will not be one of yours that you have heard before, for you have not previously destroyed me as you will encounter me in your reading of this book. The sound that you will hear is certainly not my voice since the words on this page are silent, composed as much by the white shapes around the black markings as by the markings themselves.

What I am describing is at the same time one of the most mysterious of human experiences and one of the most commonplace — it is the experience of doing battle with one's static self-identity through the recognition of a subjectivity (a human I-ness) that is other to oneself. The confrontation with alterity will not let us rest; that perception of the other I-ness once perceived will not allow us to remain who we were and we cannot rest until we have somehow come to terms with its assault on who we had been prior to being interrupted by it. This book is a disturbance, a disruption to you. You may decide to put the book down, but that would only be a postponement of something that has already been set in motion. This book has already become "an eternal curse on the reader of these pages" (Puig 1980).

If you decide not to postpone the confrontation posed by this book, you will know something of the experience of the analyst as he begins the first meeting (and every subsequent meeting) with an analysand. The analyst must be prepared to destroy and be destroyed by the otherness of the subjectivity of the analysand and to listen for a sound emerging from that collision of subjectivities that is familiar, but different from anything that he has previously heard. This listening must be done "without memory or desire" (Bion 1963), but at the same time the listener must be rooted in the history that has created (spoken) him if he is to be able to discern the sound of which I am speaking. The destruction of analyst by analysand and of analysand by analyst (as separate subjects) in the collision of subjectivities must not be complete or else the pair has fallen into the abyss of psychosis or autism. Instead, the analyst must listen to (through) the roar of the destruction from its edge, not ever being certain where that edge lies.

The subjects of analysis that will be the focus of this volume bear a dialectical relationship to one another. From the elements of the dialectic of subject and object, a new whole begins to emerge that almost immediately reveals itself to be a new source of dialectical tension. The analytic process, which creates analyst and analysand, is one in which the analysand is not simply the subject *of* analytic inquiry; the analysand at the same time must be the subject *in* that inquiry (that is, creating that inquiry) since his self-reflection is fundamental to the enterprise of psychoanalysis. Similarly, the analyst cannot simply be the observing subject of this endeavor since his subjective experience *in* this endeavor is the only possible avenue through which he gains knowledge of the relationship he is attempting to understand.

Having said something of the interdependence of analyst and analysand (as subjects creating and created, destroying and destroyed by one another), we must introduce a third term, for without it we will not have adequately described the psychoanalytic process in which the analyst and analysand as subjects of analysis create one another. The nature of the third term is that which defines the nature of psychoanalytic experience and differentiates it from all other intersubjective human events. (There exist innumerable forms of human intersubjectivity, but none involves the form of intersubjectivity that is distinctive to psychoanalysis.)

In the same moment that analyst and analysand are created, a third subject is generated that I shall refer to in this volume as the *analytic third*, since it is a middle term sustaining and sustained by the analyst and analysand as two separate subjects. More accurately, analyst and analysand come into being in the process of the creation of the analytic subject. The analytic third, although created jointly by (what is becoming) the analyst and analysand, is not experienced identically by analyst and analysand since each remains a separate subject in dialectical tension with the other. Moreover, although the analytic third is constituted in the process of the mutual negation/recognition of analyst and analysand, it does not reflect each of its creators *in the same way* any more than the third created in the experience of reading reflects the reader and writer in the same way. In other words, the transference and countertransference reflect one another, but are not mirror images of one another.

The analytic third is not only a form of experience participated in by analyst and analysand, it is at the same time a form of experiencing I-ness (a form of subjectivity) in which (through which) analyst and analysand become other than who they had been to that point. The analyst gives voice to and participates in the creation of experience that is the living past of the analysand and in this way not only hears about the analysand's experience, but *experiences his own creation of it*. The analyst does not experience the past of the analysand; rather, the analyst experiences his own creation of the past of the analysand as generated in his experience of the analytic third.

At the same time, the analysand experiences his own living past as created intersubjectively in the third. The analysand does not reexperience his past; the analysand expe-

riences his past as it is being created for the first time in the
process of its being lived in and through the analytic third. (It
is therefore a past that could be created only by this particular
analytic pair through this particular analytic third.) As an experience lived in (and through) the analytic third, onᵉ is never
completely alone with oneself (and one's past experience), since
one's experience is being created with another person. This
feature of the analytic situation creates the conditions for a
fundamental recontextualization of formerly unintegrable,
split off, unutilizable experience of the analysand.

　　To conclude (or better, to begin), psychoanalysis can be
thought of as an effort to experience, understand, and describe
the shifting nature of the dialectic generated by the creation
and negation of the analyst by the analysand and of the
analysand by the analyst *within the context of the roles constituting
the analytic set-up*. The dialectical tension generated by this
creative negation and recognition does not present a question
to be answered, a riddle to be solved. It is fitting that the riddle
of the Sphinx (taken as the paradigm of the analytic mystery of
subjectivities confronting one another) does not have *an* answer. In the myth of Oedipus, there is momentary victory for
Oedipus (and for us as audience in identification with Oedipus) in Oedipus's capacity to answer the riddle of the Sphinx
and thereby overcome the power of the Sphinx to block entry
to Thebes. But the answer to the riddle (more accurately, the
very fact that an answer was offered and was accepted) quickly
comes to strike us as a disappointing trivialization of the
question (just as Oedipus's victory over the Sphinx is ultimately revealed in the narrative to be still another reflection of
Oedipus's subjugation to the Other).

　　The question posed by the Sphinx in the form of a riddle
concerning a creature that walks on four legs in the morning,
two at midday and three in the evening, is a question about the
nature of the human condition in its multiform possibilities

(represented by fourness that becomes twoness that becomes threeness). The answer to the riddle of the Sphinx must include all possible answers to the question of what it is to be human in a community of historically rooted human beings. We must attempt not to allow the fundamental psychoanalytic questions about the nature of human experience generated in the confrontation of subjectivities in the analytic situation to be trivialized with answers that pretend to offer more than an effort to describe a moment in time that is disappearing and becoming something different as we are attempting to recognize what it is.

Each of the chapters of this volume attempts in different ways to explore a conception of psychoanalysis as a unique form of dialectical interplay of the individual subjectivities of analyst and analysand leading to the creation of a new subject (more accurately, a myriad of new subjects: the subjects of analysis).

This introductory chapter is followed by a discussion of the foundations of a psychoanalytic conception of the subject. For Freud, the subject is neither coincident with the conscious, thinking, speaking, self nor is the subject located "behind the repression barrier" in "the unconscious mind." Instead, Freud's conception of subjectivity, in my view, is fundamentally dialectical in nature and is rooted in the idea that the subject is created, maintained, and simultaneously decentered from itself through the dialectical interplay of consciousness and unconsciousness. The principle of presence-in-absence and absence-in-presence subtends the Freudian conception of this dialectical movement.

In Chapters 3 and 4, I discuss the paths by which an intersubjective conception of the subject is developed in the work of Klein and Winnicott (often in ways that they were not aware of). For Klein, the subject is constituted through the dialectical interplay of fundamentally different modes of attributing meaning to experience (the "positions") leading to the creation of a subject decentered in psychic space and in analytic time.

I view Klein's concept of projective identification (particulary as elaborated by Bion, Heimann, and H. Rosenfeld) as a monumental step in the expansion of the analytic understanding of the nature and forms of dialectical tension underlying the creation of the subject. While Freud viewed the subject as dialectically constituted in the interplay of the "qualities" of consciousness and unconsciousness, the concept of projective identification introduces a conception of the subject constituted in the context of a complex system of psychological-interpersonal forces. With the introduction of the concept of projective identification, the idea of the interdependence of subject and object became fundamental to the analytic understanding of the creation and development of subjectivity. From that point on, analytic theory of technique has undergone radical change and has become increasingly devoted over the past fifty years to the study of the interdependence of subject and object, of transference and countertransference, in human development and in the analytic process.

In the work of Winnicott, the subject is seen as coming into being in the (potential) space between mother and infant (and in the analytic space between analyst and analysand). The Winnicottian subject is generated in the context of a series of paradoxes involving forms of dialectical tension between experiences of at-one-ment and separateness, me and not-me, I and me, I and Thou. In the course of the exploration of the contributions of Klein and Winnicott to an analytic conception of the subject, I begin a discussion of the notion of a third subject created intersubjectively by the analytic pair.

In Chapter 5, the concept of the analytic third is more fully elaborated and clinically illustrated. This chapter is grounded in a detailed examination of portions of two analyses. This clinical material is provided in an effort to describe the analyst's use of his moment-to-moment experience in and of the newly created subject of analysis (the analytic third) generated jointly (but experienced differently) by the analyst and the analysand. In the first of these clinical accounts, I describe how the intersubjective experience created by the analytic pair becomes accessible to the analyst through his experience of his own "reveries" (Bion 1962a), forms of psychological activity that at first appear to be nothing more than his own distractedness, narcissistic ruminations, daydreaming, self-absorption, and the like. In the second clinical vignette, I discuss an instance in which the analyst's somatic delusion in conjunction with the analysand's sensory experiences and body-related fantasies constituted a significant medium through which the analyst came to understand the leading transference-countertransference anxieties of the phase of analysis in which these phenomena occurred.

In Chapter 6, I discuss the phenomenon of projective identification as a specific form of analytic thirdness in which the interplay of mutual subjugation and mutual recognition is fundamental to its elaboration and "analytic resolution." Projective identification is understood as a psychological-interpersonal process in which there is a partial collapse of the dialectic of subjectivity and intersubjectivity. The form of intersubjective third that is generated in projective identification is one in which the individual subjectivities of analyst and analysand (to a degree and for a time) are subsumed in (subjugated by) the newly created analytic third. A successful analytic process requires a superseding of the subjugating third and a reappropriation of the subjectivities of analyst and analysand as separate and yet interdependent individuals.

In Chapters 7 and 8, the understanding of the analytic process being discussed in this volume provides the theoretical framework for contributions to the development of two different aspects of clinical theory and analytic technique. In Chapter 7, the concept of interpretive action is explored. Interpretive action is viewed as an important, and yet little recognized, form of interpretation of the transference-countertransference. This type of interpretation (interpretation in the form of action) is understood as the analyst's use of action (other than verbally symbolic speech) to convey to the analysand specific aspects of his understanding of the transference-countertransference, which understanding cannot at that juncture in the analysis be conveyed by the semantic content of words alone. An interpretation-in-action accrues its specificity of meaning from the experiential context of the analytic intersubjectivity in which it is generated.

The development in clinical theory and technique that is addressed in Chapter 8 is the analysis of the matrix of the transference-countertransference. Here, I demonstrate the central importance of the understanding and interpretation of the matrix (or background experiential state) within which the transference-countertransference is generated. The matrix of the transference-countertransference is conceived of as the intersubjective correlate (created in the analytic setting) of the psychic space in which the patient lives. In the clinical illustrations that are presented, there is a focus on the ways in which the analyst's interpretations must often be directed at the contextual level, or matrix, of transference-countertransference (for example, the significance of the way in which the analysand is speaking, thinking, behaving, experiencing sensation, and so on, as opposed to the content of what he is saying).

Chapter 9 addresses the phenomenon of personal isolation. Pathological autism is viewed as a form of breakdown of the dialectic of subjectivity and intersubjectivity in the early mother–infant relationship. Under such circumstances, there is a failure of the mother–infant dyad to create a fluid form of intersubjectivity in which there is a balance between being in the mother-as-environment and withdrawal into autosensuality. While in healthy development there are temporary disconnections from the mother (both as object and as environment), pathological autism is conceived of as representing the complete breakdown of the intersubjectivity of mother and infant and the creation of an experience of impenetrable, uninterrupted, nonbeing.

In Chapter 10, a wide range of issues of psychoanalytic theory and practice are discussed, ranging from the timing of interpretations of the transference-countertransference in the initial analytic meeting to a discussion of contrasting conceptions of the relationship of sexuality and object relations held by different schools of analytic thought. The leitmotif of the discussion in the concluding chapter (and in the book as a whole) is a fascination with the myriad forms of interplay of individual experience and shared experience that one encounters at every level of analytic practice, from the dynamic interplay of subjectivity and intersubjectivity in the analytic hour to the relationship of the analyst (in the "present moment of the past") to the history of the development of analytic ideas.

2

The Freudian Subject

In the first moments of the opening scene of *Hamlet,* a sound is heard coming from the darkness outside the palace walls. The guard demands, "Who's there?" Like an opening dystonic chord of a piece of music, the question, "Who's there?" reverberates in an unresolved way throughout the play. The same question could be said to be the opening theme that continues unresolved through the history of psychoanalysis. Beginning with Freud and Breuer's (1893–1895) observations in *Studies on Hysteria,* the theme of the "splitting of consciousness" (p. 12) and the question of the location of the subject within this "dual consciousness" has reverberated through the succeeding century of analytic thought.

It might be surmised that Freud's limited use of the terms *self* and *subject* is a matter of semantics since Freud used the term *Das Ich* (poorly translated as *the ego*) to refer in part to the experiencing subject, "the I." However, as will be discussed, *Das Ich* is not coincident with the subject and in fact it is precisely in the difference between the two that one begins to be able to discern the creation of a new conceptual entity: the psychoanalytic subject.

It is my belief that central among the irreducible elements that define a psychoanalytic understanding of man is Freud's conception of the subject. Despite the central importance of this theme, it remained a largely implicit one in Freud's writing. As will be discussed, the implicit Freudian conception of the process by which the subject is constituted is fundamentally dialectical (Hegel 1807, Kojève 1934–1935) in nature and involves the notion that the subject is created, sustained, and at the same time decentered through the dialectical interplay of consciousness and unconsciousness.

Dialectic is a process in which opposing elements each create, preserve, and negate the other; each stands in a dynamic, ever-changing relationship to the other. Dialectical movement tends toward integrations that are never achieved. Each potential integration creates a new form of opposition characterized by its own distinct form of dialectical tension. That which is generated dialectically is continuously in motion, perpetually in the process of being created and negated, perpetually in the process of being decentered from static self-evidence. In addition, dialectical thinking involves a conception of the interdependence of subject and object: "Dialectical thought . . . [is] a process in which subject and object are so joined that truth can be determined only within the subject-object totality" (Marcuse 1960, p. viii). One cannot begin to comprehend either subject or object in isolation from one another.

When I speak of the subject of psychoanalysis, I am referring to the individual in his capacity to generate a sense of experiencing "I-ness" (subjectivity), however rudimentary and nonverbally symbolized that sense of I-ness might be. It is beyond the scope of this discussion to review the vast literature bearing on the concept of the psychoanalytic subject, which includes much of the analytic discourse addressing the concepts of the ego, the self, identity, narcissism, and so on. In addition to the works that are discussed and referred to in this and the next two chapters, the following represents a partial listing of pivotal contributions to the development of an analytic conception of the subject: Bollas (1987), Erikson (1950), Fairbairn (1952), Federn (1952), Grossman (1982), Grotstein (1981), Grunberger (1971), Guntrip (1969), Jacobson (1964), Khan (1974), Kohut (1971), Lichtenstein (1963), Loewald (1980), Mitchell (1991), Sandler (1987), Spence (1987), and Stern (1985).

Throughout his work, one can sense Freud's struggle with the limitations of the linearity of thought demanded by positivistic notions of causality. Nowhere is this more evident than in his effort to grapple with the problem of the conceptualization of the experiencing subject. Examples of Freud's attempts to formulate his ideas in linear, diachronic terms are legion and span his entire opus (see, for example, Freud's formulation of his ideas concerning the progression from unconsciousness to consciousness [1893–1895, 1900, 1909, 1923, 1925a, 1927, 1933], from the pleasure principle to the reality principle [1915a, 1930], from id to ego [1923, 1926a, 1940], from primary process to secondary process thinking [1911, 1915b]). Such linearity of thought obscures what I believe to be the radical nature of the psychoanalytic project, that is, the notion that the experiencing subject can be conceptualized as the outcome of an ongoing process in which the subject is simultaneously constituted and decentered from itself by means of the negating and preserving dialectical interplay of consciousness and unconsciousness.[1]

_____

1. When I use the term *consciousness,* I am referring to Freud's System Preconscious-Conscious, and when I use the term *unconsciousness,* I am referring to an order of experience referred to by Freud as the dynamic

In this and the following two chapters, I shall discuss aspects of the concept of the dialectically constituted and decentered subject of psychoanalysis that have their origins in the work of Freud and that were developed by Klein and Winnicott. In this effort, I shall define what I consider to be some of the central dialectics bearing on the constitution of the subject introduced by Freud, Klein, and Winnicott. In addressing the work of Klein and Winnicott, I shall focus in particular on the development of a conception of an intersubjective context for the creation of individual subjectivity.

Freud's Decentering of Man from Consciousness

Freud (1917) believed that psychoanalysis presented a reconceptualization of man's relationship to himself that involved a fundamental decentering of man from himself. Man, according to Freud (1916–1917), has been decentered in three different ways in the course of modern history. First, the Copernican revolution effected the displacement of man from his position at "the stationary centre of the universe, with the sun, moon and planets circling round it" (1917, p. 139). Second, the Darwinian restructuring of our conception of the biological world resulted in man's dislocation from the position that he had created for himself as "different from animals" (p.

---

unconscious or the System Unconscious. The latter order of experience is not only devoid of the quality of self-awareness, but is comprised of a set of meanings that are felt to be incompatible with, unacceptable to, and threatening to the system of meanings constituted in consciousness. In addition, the two orders of experience (the System Unconscious and the System Preconscious-Conscious) are characterized by different "principles of mental functioning" (Freud 1911), that is, different forms of psychic representation, different rules of psychic transformation, different types of temporality, and so on.

141) and holding a divinely ordained position above and separate from them. The third and by far the most disturbing form of decentering of man was effected by psychoanalysis, which decentered man from himself by undermining the illusion of the identity of consciousness and mind.

From a psychoanalytic perspective, man can no longer experience himself as "absolute ruler" (1917, p. 143) of his own mind: *"the ego is not master in its own house"* (p. 143). "'Come, let yourself be taught something on this one point! What is in your mind does not coincide with what you are conscious of'" (1917, p. 143). The ego (the I), especially in its claim to sovereignty through its capacity for self-consciousness, perception, speech, motility, and so on, believes that it knows itself: "'You [the ego] feel sure that you are informed of all that goes on in your mind . . . Indeed, you go so far as to regard what is "mental" as identical with what is "conscious"'" (1917, pp. 142–143). The thinking, feeling, behaving, speaking subject is decentered from the self-evidence of his experience of consciousness. "Thoughts emerge suddenly without one's knowing where they come from, nor can one do anything to drive them away. These alien guests even seem to be more powerful than those which are at the ego's command" (1917, p. 141).

The subject in the historical era of psychoanalysis is no longer to be considered coincident with conscious awareness, no longer to be equated with the conscious, speaking, behaving, "I" (ego).

The Freudian decentering of the subject from consciousness by no means represents a simple transposition of the subject to a position behind the repression barrier. The psychoanalytic subject is not relocated from consciousness to the unconscious mind (in the topographic model), or to the id (in the structural model). Rather, Freud (1940) emphasized that consciousness and unconsciousness must be conceived as "[coexisting] qualities of what is psychical" (p. 161). Neither

consciousness nor unconsciousness in themselves represents
the subject of psychoanalysis. The subject for Freud is to be
sought in the phenomenology corresponding to that which lies
in the relations *between* consciousness and unconsciousness.

The Dialectic of Consciousness and Unconsciousness

Freud by no means conceived of the unconscious mind as
the seat of truth or as the locus of man's soul. He recognized
that the claims of the unconscious to know and to constitute
the totality of the subject are as ill-founded as those of the
conscious, speaking subject. He neither romanticized the
unconscious as the residue of "natural man" (untainted by
civilization), nor did he villainize the unconscious by viewing it
as the source of sin, the wellspring of depraved lust and
viciousness. Consciousness and unconsciousness are conceived
of as mutually dependent, each defining, negating, and preserving the other. Neither exists nor has any conceptual or
phenomenological meaning except in relation to the other. The
two "co-intend" (Ricoeur 1970, p. 378) in a relationship of
relative difference as opposed to absolute difference; the two
coexist in a mutually defining relationship of difference.

It is critical to Freud's argument that conscious and
unconscious experience be conceived of as qualities of experience that are created in a discourse (a "communication" [Freud
1915b, p. 190]) between the two. By means of the discourse
between conscious and unconscious qualities of experience, the
illusion (or virtual image [Freud 1940, p. 145]) of unity of
experience is created. The discourse of consciousness and
unconsciousness is guaranteed by the principle of continuity
and difference between the two coexisting modes of generating

experience. The attribute of "being conscious [*Bewusstheit*] . . .
forms the point of departure for all our investigations" (Freud
1915b, p. 172) and, as will be seen, is also the point to which
all of our investigations return.

Not only is discourse possible between unconsciousness
and consciousness, the very existence of each depends upon the
other: "In themselves [unconscious processes] cannot be
cognized, indeed are even incapable of carrying on their
existence [independent of the System Preconscious-Con-
scious]" (Freud 1915b, p. 187). The relationship between the
two systems is that of a specific form of discourse, a discourse
of a dialectical nature in which the components are comparable
to empty sets each filled by the other (Ogden 1986, 1989a).
Each constitutes a presence affirmed by its absence in the
other. The System Unconscious is the Other to the System
Preconscious-Conscious and the System Preconscious-Conscious is the negating, preserving Other to the System Unconscious. In Freud's schema, neither consciousness nor
(dynamic) unconsciousness holds a privileged position in relation to the other: the two systems are "complementary" (Freud
1940, p. 159) to one another thus constituting a single, but
divided discourse.

Freud (1915b) felt that the term *subconscious* is "incorrect
and misleading" (p. 170) in that the Unconscious does not exist
"under" consciousness; there is only one mental life comprised
of the product of the interplay of (dynamically) unconscious
and conscious psychical qualities. In other words, we do not
live two lives (a conscious and an unconscious one) concur-
rently; we live a single life constituted by the interplay of the
conscious and (dynamically) unconscious aspects of experience.

The System Unconscious is not only incapable of carrying on life without access to perception, speech, motility, and
so on, all of which are linked to the System Preconscious-

Conscious. Far more fundamental to an understanding of the psyche is the idea that unconsciousness is without meaning except in relation to the concept of consciousness, and vice versa. Unconsciousness cannot be described except by means of a series of statements of negations of qualities of consciousness, beginning with the very name given to each. Each of the qualities of the System Unconscious (for example, exemption from mutual contradiction, timelessness, replacement of external by psychic reality, lack of fixity of cathexis) is delineated as a concept by virtue of its relationship of negation to a concept defining the system Preconscious-Conscious.

Freud's (1923) structural model represents a system of dialectics built upon (and by no means replacing) the topographic model. In the structural model, the mind is conceived of in terms of mutually defining dialectics constituted by the ego (the I), the id (it that is not me and yet within me), and the superego (that part of me that lords over me threateningly and protectively). The decentering of the subject in the structural model is not different in kind from that which has been discussed in relation to the topographic model. The subject is no more coincident with the ego of the structural model than it is coincident with consciousness in the topographic model. The subject of the structural model is located in the dialectically constituted stereoscopic illusion of unity of experience constituted by the negating and preserving discourse of the id, ego, and superego.

The Dialectic of Presence and Absence

I shall now focus more closely on the principle of presence in absence and absence in presence, a concept that lies at the

heart of the Freudian conception of the dialectically constitu-
ted/decentered subject. This principle subtends the dialectical
movement between mutually negating and preserving dimensions of experience. Presence is continually negated by that
which it is not, while all the time alluding to what is lacking in
itself. That which is absent is always present in the lack that it
presents.

Freud's (1925b) "Negation" paper presents a subtle,
highly condensed statement of the dialectical relationship of
presence and absence, affirmation and negation: "the content
of a repressed image or idea can make its way into consciousness, on condition that it is *negated*. Negation is a way of taking
cognizance of what is repressed [what cannot be given cognizance consciously]; indeed, it is already a lifting [*Aufhebung*] of
the repression, though not, of course, an acceptance of what is
repressed" (1925b, pp. 235-236). Thus, in negation, the
repression is "lifted," and yet what is repressed is not accepted.

Hyppolite (1956) has pointed out that *Aufhebung* "is
Hegel's dialectical word, which means simultaneously to deny,
to suppress and to conserve, and fundamentally to raise up" (p.
291). The use of the word *Aufhebung* underscores that repression must not be understood as a linear movement from
consciousness to unconsciousness. Freud's concept of negation
represents a distinctively psychoanalytic conception of the
constitution of the subject. The idea of a dialectic of affirmed
and disavowed meaning played out phenomenologically in the
form of the simultaneity of conscious and unconscious
meaning is perhaps the most fundamental analytic proposition
concerning the concept of mind. "Presenting one's being in the
mode of not being it, that is truly what is at issue in this
Aufhebung of the repression, which is not an acceptance of what
is repressed. The person speaking says: 'This is what I am not'"
(Hyppolite 1956, p. 291).

Clinical Illustration

The following brief clinical vignette may serve to illustrate something of the phenomenology of the dialectic of consciousness and unconsciousness, of presence and absence, of affirmation and negation upon which the analytic enterprise rests.

> An analysand, Mr. M., began an analytic hour with a 10-minute silence that was followed by a series of highly articulate, but affectless self-reflections. I said to him that I wondered whether something might have occurred during yesterday's meeting that was leading him to talk in such a detached way.[2] The patient replied that while in the waiting room, he had been trying to remember what we had been talking about at the end of yesterday's meeting and was feeling stupid and clumsy for not being able to remember. It felt as if something had been left unfinished. I said that it had been important enough for him to forget. Mr. M. said that his not being able to remember felt like a hole in him; it was not only frustrating, it was frightening to know that something had happened and not to be able to know what it was.
>
> This feeling of the present absence reflected not only the existence of dynamically unconscious experience, but also reflected the specific nature of that unconscious experience. At the end of the previous meeting, the patient had been talking about the way in which as a child he had tenaciously insisted on wearing clothes that reflected his own taste, for example, wearing green-brown

---

2. Boyer (1988) has discussed the way in which the principal unresolved transference–countertransference anxiety of a given analytic hour constitutes a primary unconscious context for the subsequent meeting.

loafers as opposed to the plain brown ones that were prescribed by the school dress code. Mr. M. had begun to understand this as a response to a feeling that his mother (a schizoid woman) was unable to recognize that he had a personality of his own that was characterized by his own specific likes, dislikes, fears, hatreds, jealousies, competitiveness, and so on. (The patient had previously mentioned that his mother each year bought the same Christmas present for all four of her children.) Enacted in the patient's forgetting in the current analytic hour was an effort to determine if I would be able to remember what it was that had occurred in the previous meeting, thereby reflecting my own capacity to distinguish him from everyone else in my life.

I said to Mr. M. that I thought he was worried that I would not be able to remember our previous meeting. He was surprised by this comment and said that remembering seemed too personal a thing to expect of me. He had had a vague sense that I wrote things down and that I referred to them when I needed to.

The patient's fear that I would not remember him, his wish for recognition, his anxiety about asking me directly for such recognition, and his anger connected with the feeling that in the past I had failed to recognize him and would certainly do so again today, were all present in the absence of affect and memory (and in the experience of there being something missing). What was present was an affirmation of all that was absent. Thus, that which was missing was experientially present (the conscious experience of the hole in himself) and that which was present was absent (the fantasy of me as mechanical that the patient became aware of after I interpreted his anxiety).

The psychoanalytic method as developed by Freud is built upon the process of constituting meaning through this type of dialectic of presence in absence and absence in presence. It would be inaccurate to say that Mr. M. was not feeling anger, loneliness, the wish to be recognized, and the fear of not being recognized. It would be equally inaccurate to say that he was "really" experiencing such thoughts and feelings in his "unconscious mind." Both statements in themselves reflect forms of reductionism that fail to capture the phenomenology of dialectically constituted experience. The psychoanalytic conception of the nature of experience requires that any full statement of the patient's experience be framed dialectically in a way that acknowledges the mutually negating and preserving contextualization of presence by absence and of absence by presence. The concept of transference itself represents a dialectical conception of a past that is present and a present that is past.

Similarily, the analytic understanding of dream experience is built upon this dialectic of presence and absence; the latent dream content is not the solution to the riddle of the manifest dream. The phenomenology of dreaming is one that hovers between the visible and the invisible, the presented and the unpresented, the narrative text and the silent text. Presence and absence stand in an unending process of mutual affirmation and negation that prevents dream experience from ever lighting in any given locale. When one has "figured out" the meaning of a dream, one has lost touch with the aliveness and elusiveness of the experience of dreaming; in its place one has created a flat, bloodless decoded message.

The Language of the Subject

From the perspective of the foregoing discussion, I would like to briefly comment on an aspect of psychoanalytic language. I believe that a psychoanalytic theory of experiencing "I-ness" must incorporate into its own structure and language a recognition of the ineffable, constantly moving and evolving nature of subjectivity (described by Kundera [1984] as "the unbearable lightness of being"). I have elected to use the term *subject* in this discussion to refer to the individual in his ever-changing dialectically negating and negated experience of "I-ness" instead of either the term *self* or the term *ego*.

Although the term *self* is indispensable in the description of aspects of the phenomenology of subjectivity (for instance, in describing the individual's sense of who he is or the experience of "me-ness" as the sense of self-as-object), I feel that the term *self* as a theoretical construct has become weighted down with static, reifying meanings. The concept of self is often used in a way that seems to designate a localizable entity "inside" the person. This is particularly true when the self is conceived of as a "psychic structure" (Kohut 1971, p. xv), "a content of the mental apparatus" (p. xv) with a "psychic location" (p. xv). When used in this way, the term *self* is poorly suited to convey a sense of "I-ness" emerging from a continually decentering dialectical process.

Spruiell (1981) has elegantly argued that the term *ego* when used in the sense that Freud employed *Das Ich* (i.e., to refer to the person as well as to a psychological system) is sufficiently flexible and ambiguous to encompass both the experiential and the metapsychological "I." However, the term *ego* is significantly different from Freud's far more personal term *Das Ich* (the "I"). Freud (1926b) specifically cautioned against the use of "orotund Greek names" (p. 195) for *Das Ich* in order to "keep [psychoanalytic concepts] in contact with the popular mode of thinking" (p. 195). Particularly when used to refer to a group of psychic functions, the term *ego* loses virtually all connection with the phenomenology of the experience of "I-ness" and becomes almost entirely a metapsychological abstraction (see for example, Hartmann 1950, Hartmann et al. 1946, Loewenstein 1967).

Moreover, even Freud's term, *Das Ich,* chosen with the intention of keeping analytic discourse regarding the mind close to the everyday "I," refers to only one aspect of the psyche. In the topographical model, Freud was clear that *Das Ich* (the ego) is not "master in its own house" and therefore must not be equated with the psychoanalytic conception of the mind as a whole that necessarily includes that which is not the ego, that is, the Unconscious, that which stands in tension with, in "communication" with, the thinking, feeling, conscious, speaking "I."

As I have discussed above, in the structural model, *Das Ich* is no more coincident with the psyche than is consciousness in the topographic model. *Das Ich* in the structural model stands in a mutually preserving and negating relationship to *Das Es* (the it). The "it" is not "I" and yet in health is inextricably part of what is in the process of becoming "I" and a part of what I am becoming ("*Wo Es war, soll Ich werden*": "Where id [it] was, there ego [I] shall be," [Freud 1933, p. 80]). To equate *Das Ich* (the ego of the structural model) with the experiencing "I" is to obscure the generative process of mutual negation and preservation involving ego, id, and superego upon which the structural model is based. To make such an equation is to mistake the part (the ego) for the dialectical (negating and negated) whole.

Although no single word can carry the requisite multiplicity, ambiguity, and specificity of meaning, the term *subject* seems particularly well suited to convey the psychoanalytic conception of the experiencing "I" in both a phenomenological and a metapsychological sense. The term is etymologically linked with the word *subjectivity* and carries an inherent semantic reflexivity, that is, it simultaneously denotes subject and object, I and it, I and me. The word *subject* refers to both

The subject 'me' is observed by the object 'I'

the "I" as speaker, thinker, writer, reader, perceiver, and so on, and to the object of subjectivity, that is, to the topic (the subject) being discussed, the idea being contemplated, the percept being viewed, and so on. As a result, the subject can never be fully separated from the object and therefore can never be completely centered in itself. As will be discussed in the next two chapters, the reflexivity of the dialectic of subject and object is a fundamental component of the evolving psychoanalytic conception of the decentered experiencing "I."

Concluding Comments

Freud proposed a model of the mind in which there is no privileged position in which to locate the subject either in consciousness or in the realm of the dynamically unconscious. Instead the subject is constituted by psychical acts that have qualities of consciousness and the absence of consciousness. Each is reflected through the other; each is negated by the other. Every way of being conscious is undercut by the unconscious with which it is "co-implicit" (Ricoeur 1970, p. 378) or "co-intended" (p. 378); every way of being unconscious is experienced through its effects on consciousness, that is, on the way in which perceptible, consciously registered experience is shaped, interrupted, intensified, lacunized, contextualized, and so on. Although the Freudian decentering of the subject begins with the overcoming of the ego's presumption of mastery of its own house, we must always begin with and return to consciousness in some form in our investigations since it is only through that which we can perceive that we feel the effects of that which lacks the quality of consciousness. However alien the unconscious may seem, the continuity between the System Unconscious and the System Precon-

scious-Conscious is maintained in that both pertain to the same
system of human meaning (although not necessarily in the
same symbolic form).

A Postscript on Lacan

A full discussion of the Lacanian conception of the subject is
not possible within the space of the present chapter. However,
before addressing the Kleinian and Winnicottian elaborations
of Freud's conception of the subject in the two following
chapters, I would like to note briefly that despite the fact that
there are large areas of convergence of thought in the work of
Freud, Klein, Winnicott, and Lacan, I view the Lacanian
project as differing in fundamental ways from the lines of
thought being traced through the work of Freud, Klein, and
Winnicott. The latter three analysts worked entirely within a
dialectical, hermeneutic framework wherein the analytic dialogue (as well as the intrapersonal dialogue) is based on a
mutually interpretive discourse in which meanings are clarified
and elaborated and in which enhanced understandings of the
experience of oneself and the other are generated (Habermas
1968). For Lacan also, the understanding of the analytic
process and of the constitution and decentering of the subject
is informed by dialectical thought, for example, Lacan's (1957)
conception of the nature of the interplay of the registers of the
Imaginary, the Symbolic, and the Real, and his understanding
of the nature of the interdependence of subject and object
in the analytic transference-countertransference relationship
(Lacan 1951).

However, there is, alongside and in tension with the
dialectical components of Lacan's work, a significant decon-
structionist element in the Lacanian project that is not present

in the work of Freud, Klein, and Winnicott. For Lacan (1966a), there is a radical splitting between signifier and signified such that the chain of signifiers (the set of sound elements of language) is perpetually "sliding" over the signified (the set of concepts generated by language). This disjunction makes the "interval" (the break) the most fundamental structure of the signifying chain (Lacan 1966b). Thus, the meanings we create through language are inevitably built upon misnamings, misrecognitions that we rely upon to create the illusion of understanding. These meanings do not have the same status as the Freudian manifest content from which chains of associations are generated and which allow increasingly rich contextualization and enhanced understandings of "co-implicit" conscious and unconscious meanings. In Lacanian thinking, the manifest text must to a large degree be deconstructed in order to avoid endlessly circling in its misrecognitions. Slips, errors, witticisms, word plays, symptomatic acts, and so on provide "intervals" (Lacan 1966b) (as opposed to the interplay of creatively negating contexts) through which to glimpse that which is unintended by the speaking subject.

The Lacanian project can be likened to an effort to see through the intervals or chips in the surface presentation of a painting over a painting. In contrast, the Freudian project can be conceived of in terms of the hermeneutic circle in which foreground is contextualized by background and vice versa; the Freudian text is assumed to have an integrity in which every part is related to, informs, and is informed by every other part of the text. There is no radical discontinuity among portions of the fabric of meaning whether conscious or unconscious, manifest or latent, intended or "unintended." In fact, the notion of the unintended is without meaning from the perspective of Freud's view of the relationship of the parts to the whole. The "unintended" is more accurately termed the "co-intended" (Ricoeur 1970). The fundamental logic under-

lying the discordant elements of the text is the logic of the
dialectical interplay of presence and absence discussed above.

A major outcome of the Lacanian notion of the radical
disjunction of signifier and signified is the conception of the
deconstructed subject that emerges from his work. The unconscious is constituted by the chain of signifiers, the Other. The
subject is spoken by the Other and is in that sense "without a
head" ("*acéphale*," Lacan 1954–1955). A radical disjunction
separates the subject of the unconscious (that which is spoken
by the Other, the chain of signifiers) from the self-conscious
(misrecognizing and misnaming) speaking subject. The two
orders of meaning and subjectivity do not constitute a dialectical whole. Rather, the Lacanian subject is not simply decentered, but is radically disconnected from itself leaving a central
"lack" or void resulting from the fact that the speaking subject
and the subject of the unconscious are irrevocably divided by
the unbridgeable gap separating signifier and signified.

Summary

Central among the irreducible elements that define a psychoanalytic understanding of man is Freud's conception of the
subject, and yet this theme remained a largely implicit one in
Freud's writing. The Freudian conception of the process by
which the subject is constituted is fundamentally dialectical in
nature and involves the notion that the subject is created and
sustained (and at the same time decentered from itself)
through the dialectical interplay of consciousness and unconsciousness.

The contribution of psychoanalysis to a theory of subjectivity involves the formulation of a concept of the subject in
which neither consciousness nor unconsciousness holds a priv-

ileged position in relation to the other; the two coexist in a mutually creating, preserving, and negating relationship to one another. The principle of presence-in-absence and absence-in-presence subtends the dialectical movement between conscious and unconscious dimensions of subjectivity.

3

Toward an Intersubjective Conception of the Subject: The Kleinian Contribution

Psychoanalytic thought emerging from the British School has contributed in significant ways to the elaboration of the concept of the dialectically constituted (and decentered) subject. Having discussed the Freudian conception of the subject in the previous chapter, I shall now explore the Kleinian contribution to this project. Chapter 4 discusses the Winnicottian contribution.

Three of the most important of Melanie Klein's theoretical contributions to the development of an analytic formulation of subjectivity are (1) the dialectical conception of psychic structure and psychological development underlying her concept of "positions," (2) the dialectical decentering of the subject in psychic space, and (3) the notion of the dialectic of intersubjectivity that is implicit in the concept of projective identification. Klein's attention was not focused on the theoretical question of the nature of subjectivity and as a result, we, as interpreters of her work, may be a better position than

Klein herself to understand the place of her thinking in the development of the psychoanalytic conception of the subject.

The Dialectical Interplay of Psychic Organizations

Klein's (1935) notion of *positions* is fundamentally different from the concepts of developmental stages and developmental phases. The latter concepts are linear in nature with one phase or stage following, building upon, and integrating those that preceded it. Klein's positions do not refer to periods of development through which one passes on the way to psychological maturity: "I chose the term 'position' . . . because these groupings of anxieties and defences, although arising first during the earliest stages [of life], are not restricted to them" (Klein 1952a, p. 93).

Positions neither follow nor precede one another; rather, each coexists with the others in a dialectical relationship (Ogden 1988). Just as the concept of the conscious mind is without meaning except in relation to the concept of the unconscious mind, each of the Kleinian positions is without meaning except in relation to one another. The Kleinian subject exists not in any given position or hierarchical layering of positions, but in the dialectical tension created *between* positions.

The forms of experience associated with the paranoid-schizoid position (Klein 1946, 1952a) and the depressive position (Klein 1935, 1948, 1952a) can only be named by referring to the ways in which each represents a pole of the dialectical process in which each creates, negates, and preserves the other. I understand the Kleinian positions as psychological organizations that determine the ways in which meaning is attributed to experience (see Ogden 1986, 1989a). Associated with each of the positions is a particular quality of anxiety, forms of defense and object relatedness, a type of symbolization, and a quality of subjectivity. Together these qualities of experience constitute a state of being that characterizes each of the positions.

From the perspective of a conceptualization of the Kleinian idea of positions as poles of a dialectical process through which the subject is constituted, each of the positions is understood as a fiction, a nonexistent ideal that is never encountered in pure form. Nonetheless, for purposes of clarity of discussion, I shall present a highly schematized view of each of the positions as if each could be isolated from the others.

The paranoid-schizoid position represents a psychological organization generating a state of being that is ahistorical, relatively devoid of the experience of an interpreting subject mediating between the sense of I-ness and one's lived sensory experience, part-object related, and heavily reliant on splitting, idealization, denial, projective identification, and omnipotent thinking as modes of defense and ways of organizing experience. This paranoid-schizoid mode contributes to the sense of immediacy and intensity of experience.

The depressive pole of the dialectic of modes of generating experience (i.e., the depressive position) is characterized by (1) an experience of interpreting "I-ness" mediating between onself and one's lived sensory experience; (2) the presence of an historically rooted sense of self that is continuous over time and over shifts in affective states; (3) relatedness to other people who are experienced as whole and separate subjects with an internal life similar to one's own; moreover, one is able to feel concern for the Other, guilt, and the wish to make nonmagical reparation for the real and imagined damage that one has done to others; and (4) forms of defense (e.g., repression and mature identification) that allow the individual to sustain psychological strain over time (as opposed to relying upon somatization, fragmentation, or evacuative phantasies and enactments as means of dissipating and foreclosing psychic pain). In sum, the depressive mode generates a quality of experience endowed with a richness of layered symbolic meanings.

I have elsewhere (1988, 1989a) introduced my own conception of a third pole of the dialectic constituting human experience: the autistic-contiguous position. The autistic-contiguous position is conceived of as a psychological organization that is more primitive than the positions delineated by Klein. Such a conception represents an elaboration and extension of the work of Bick (1968, 1986), Meltzer (1975, Meltzer et al. 1975) and Tustin (1972, 1980, 1984, 1990). The autistic-contiguous position is associated with a mode of generating experience that is of a sensation-dominated sort and is characterized by protosymbolic impressions of sensory experience that together help constitute an experience of bounded surfaces. Rhythmicity and experiences of sensory contiguity (especially at the skin surface) contribute to an elemental sense of continuity of being over time. Such experiences are generated within the invisible matrix of the environmental mother. Relationships with objects (that are not experienced as objects) occur in the form of experiences of "auto-sensuous shapes" (Tustin 1984) and "auto-sensuous objects" (Tustin 1990). These idiosyncratic, but organized and organizing uses of sensory experiences of softness and hardness represent facets of the process by which the sensory floor of all experience is generated.

It must be emphasized that the negating and preserving interplay of positions evolves along a diachronic (temporally sequential) axis as well as a synchronic one. The interplay of diachronicity and synchronicity represents an inextricable component of the dialectical nature of the concept of positions. A psychological theory becomes untenable if it does not incorporate a recognition of the directionality of time and of life. It would be absurd to adopt an exclusively synchronic perspective that fails to recognize the progression of states of maturity that takes place in the course of the life of the individual. To undervalue the importance of the diachronic axis in Kleinian theory would be to obscure the developmental significance (both in the course of maturation and during analysis) of critical moments or periods of psychic reorganization such as those involved in the achievement of a more fully elaborated depressive position, for example, as reflected in the development of the individual's capacity for guilt, mourning, empathy, gratitude, and so on. On the other hand, a psychological theory that overvalues the diachronic (e.g., an over-reliance on the concept of the developmental line) at the expense of the synchronic, tends to ignore the importance of the primitive dimension of all experience including those forms of experience considered to be the most mature and fully evolved.

There are many instances in Klein's writing where the concept of position seems to shift from a dialectical conception (recognizing the coexistence and mutual contextualization of positions) to a linear one. For example, Klein (1948, 1952a) regularly described the paranoid-schizoid position as being associated with the first quarter of the first year of life while portraying the depressive position as having its origins in the second quarter of the first year of life. There is a telling passage in which Klein (1952a) states that the paranoid-schizoid and depressive positions arise very early in development and "*recur* during the first years of childhood and *under certain circumstances* in later life" (p. 93, italics added). The idea that these fundamental positions "recur" in childhood and then "under certain circumstances" throughout life represents a reversion to a linear model of development in which positions are conceived of as early stages with fixation points to which the individual regresses in states of psychological illness or strain. Such a view is entirely inconsistent with Klein's larger view of positions as ever-present psychological organizations whose relationship shifts not by means of succession or progression from one to another, but by means of shifts in the way in which each contextualizes the others.

Klein's dialectical conception of psychic structure and its development fully incorporates an appreciation of Freud's notion of the timelessness of the unconscious. Freud's (1911, 1915b) conception of the timelessness of the unconscious dimension of experience established the notion of the individual existing simultaneously within two forms of time — diachronic (linear, sequential) time and synchronic time. Each form of time has its own validity in the context of its own psychic system (the System Preconscious-Conscious and the System Unconscious). The psychoanalytic subject is therefore dialectically constituted (simultaneously) within and outside of diachronic, consensually measured time.

The Kleinian dialectical conception of psychic structure and psychological development effects a decentering of the subject from his position at the "front" of a developmental line. Instead, the subject is conceived of as existing in psychoanalytic time (as opposed to linear, sequential time), thus partaking of all facets of subjectivity and all forms of primitivity and maturity, simultaneously and in shifting interrelatedness. Psychoanalytic infancy is not restricted to the earliest months of life; instead, the notion of the timelessness of the unconscious requires that we view the autistic-contiguous, the paranoid-schizoid, and the depressive positions as together constituting facets of time present in every period of life. The depressive position is not to be understood as a reflection of the successful negotiation of the conflicts and anxieties of the autistic-contiguous and paranoid-schizoid positions; rather, the depressive position is a component of psychological life from the very beginning (for example, in the infant's confrontation with otherness in his distress at the moment of birth).

Even before Klein introduced the concept of position, she had begun to challenge the idea of the individual's rootedness in developmental, linear time (Klein 1932). She suggested that genital excitation, desire, and phantasy (including oedipal phantasies) coexist with the "earlier" (i.e., oral, anal, and urethal) libidinal tendencies. "Displacement" (Klein 1932) or "spreading" (Bibring 1947, p. 73) of libidinal excitation and its attendant unconscious desires and object-related phantasies call into play "all [aspects of libidinal development] at the same time" (Klein 1932, p. 272).

It might be said that Klein has contributed to the compounding of man's third historical decentering, the psychological decentering of man from his own consciousness. A dialectical conception of psychic structure and its development displaces man from his position at the leading edge of what he believes to be his "progression" through the stages of his life: "The past is not dead: it is not even past" (Faulkner). The depressive position, despite its attributes of historicity and the capacity to create and interpret symbols, is no more the locus of the subject in Kleinian theory than is consciousness or the ego in Freudian theory.

The Dialectic of Splitting and Integration of the Subject

Having discussed the Kleinian dialectic of psychological organizations, I would now like to focus on a second contribution of Kleinian theory to the development of the concept of the dialectically constituted and decentered subject. For Klein, the psyche (after an initial hypothetical moment of unity) enters

into an ongoing process of splitting of the ego and a corresponding division of the (internal) object. The ego and object
are split into components that hold meaning for (are "cathected
by") one another. For example, the hating and hated component of the object is the facet of the (internal) object that (for
defensive purposes) holds meaning for and is recognized by the
hating and hated component of the ego. In this way, the
individual can safely hate the bad object without fear of
destroying the object that is loving and beloved.

The Kleinian subject is decentered from itself in that
none of the multiplicity of components of the ego and internal
objects is coextensive with the subject. Such a conception of
the subject as constituted in large part by a multiplicity of
phantasied internal object relationships represents an elaboration of the Freudian dispersal (decentering) of the subject over
consciousness and unconsciousness (in the topographic model)
and later among the psychic agencies (in the structural model).
Thus, the Kleinian dispersal of the subject over the full field of
phantasied internal object relations can be viewed as an
extension of the decentered Freudian subject: "The [Freudian]
intrasubjective field [as conceptualized in the structural model]
tends to be conceived of after the fashion of intersubjective
relations, and the systems are pictured as relatively autonomous persons-within-the-person (the superego, for instance, is
said to behave in a sadistic way towards the ego)" (Laplanche
and Pontalis 1967, p. 452).

The Kleinian subject is not only split (dispersed) among
the phantasied internal object relations constituting it, the
splitting process itself represents part of a dialectic of dispersal
and unity of the subject, a dialectic of fragmentation and
integration, of de-linkage and closure, of part-object relations
and whole-object relations. This dialectic of dispersal and
unity represents another facet of the relationship of the
paranoid-schizoid and depressive positions (represented by
Bion [1963] by the notation $Ps \leftrightarrow D$).

The dialectic of splitting and integration in psychological space can be thought of as having both an intrapersonal and an interpersonal facet. Intrapsychically, the splitting processes associated with the paranoid-schizoid position lead to the construction of an internal object world continuously subjected to pressures of deintegration. There exists (as a facet of the paranoid-schizoid component of the dialectic constituting experience) a movement toward the breakdown of experience into part-object relations existing in an ahistorical context wherein thoughts and feelings are experienced as forces and objects. In the extreme, such disintegrative pressures lead to intense phantasies of the explosion of the subject (thus, dispersing the internal object world throughout the entirety of unbounded space) or to phantasies of the implosion of the subject (resulting from feelings of the fragmentation of internal objects in so thorough a fashion that the subject disappears into its own internal vacuum).

It is important that one not pathologize the negating, deintegrative, decentering pressures associated with the paranoid-schizoid component of the Ps ↔ D dialectic. The intrapsychic pressure for deintegration represents an essential negation of the integrative qualities associated with the depressive pole of the dialectic. In the absence of the deintegrative pressure of the paranoid-schizoid pole of the dialectic generating experience, the integration associated with the depressive position would reach closure, stagnation, and "arrogance" (Bion 1967). The negation of closure, the "attacks on linking" (Bion 1959) represented by the paranoid-schizoid pole of the dialectic, has the effect of destabilizing that which would otherwise become static. In this way, the negating, deintegrative effects of the paranoid-schizoid position continually generate the potential for new psychological possibilities (i.e., the possibility for psychic change).

The experience of dreaming itself is a reflection of the dialectical tension between the paranoid-schizoid and depressive positions. Dreaming is not simply a process of speaking to oneself about unconscious thoughts and feelings in coded form during sleep; far more importantly, it is an experience of deintegrating one's experience and re-presenting it to oneself in a new form and in a new context (the context of the dream space). The act of re-presenting one's experience in the form of a dream constitutes the creation of a new experience, a new integration that is immediately undergoing deintegration (as reflected in the experience of the dream as a fading, ephemeral, barely knowable psychic event). At times, the dialectic of integration and deintegration underlying the experience of dreaming collapses into the terror of disintegration when one despairs about the adequacy of the containing (integrative) dimension of one's internal world. This may result in an intense fear of *falling* asleep, a fear that reflects the phantasy that one will not be "held" in sleep and will be dropped into endless, shapeless space ("when the bough breaks").

Projective Identification

Having briefly discussed the intrapsychic component of the dialectic of integration and deintegration underlying the constitution and decentering of the Kleinian subject, I shall now turn to an exploration of the interpersonal component of this dialectic. The idea of projective identification (particularly, as elaborated by Bion [1952, 1962a, 1963] and H. Rosenfeld [1965, 1971, 1987]) is the concept that most powerfully addresses the interpersonal component of the dialectic of dispersal and integration, of negation and creation of the subject in Kleinian theory.

The intersubjective dimension of the process of projective identification is suggested by Klein (1946) in her statement that in projective identification "split-off parts of the ego are also projected on to the mother, or as I would rather call it, *into* the mother . . . [in an effort] to control and to take possession of the object. . . . In so far as the mother comes to contain the bad parts of the self, she is not felt to be a separate individual but is felt to be *the* bad self" (p. 8). Thus, Klein proposes that there exists from the earliest stages of life a psychic process by which aspects of the self are not simply projected onto the psychic representation of the object (as in projection), but "*into*" the object in a way that is felt to control the object from within and leads to the projector's experiencing the object as a part of himself.

The experiential level of projective identification is presented by Klein (1955) in the form of a discussion of a novella by Julian Green, *If I Were You*. In Green's story, the protagonist, driven by envy, makes a deal with the devil wherein he trades his soul for the power to leave his own body and take possession of the body and life of anyone he chooses. Klein describes the anxiety associated with the (phantasied) experience of inhabiting the Other while at the same time attempting not to completely lose one's sense of self. (It is essential not to entirely lose oneself in the Other since the complete loss of a sense of one's rootedness in oneself is equivalent to one's disappearance and psychic death.) Projective identification, according to Klein, is psychically depleting in that an immense expenditure of energy is involved in the effort to control the Other so thoroughly that he is experienced as having taken on an aspect of one's own identity.[1]

Bion (1952, 1962a, 1963) made a number of important

---

[1]The notion of an interpersonal dimension of projective identification remained ambiguous and undeveloped in Klein's work. Bion (1952) and H. Rosenfeld (1971) pioneered the clinical exploration and theoretical formulation of projective identification as a psychological-interpersonal process.

contributions to the development of the concept of an interpersonal component of projective identification and to the beginnings of an articulation of the notion of an interpersonal
space in which subjectivity and the capacity for thinking is
created (and at times attacked). In describing the phenomenology of projective identification, Bion stated: "The analyst
feels he is being manipulated so as to be playing a part, no
matter how difficult to recognize, in somebody else's phantasy"
(1952, p. 149). Thus, projective identification for Bion is not
simply an unconscious phantasy of projecting an aspect of
oneself into the Other and controlling him from within; it
represents a psychological-interpersonal event in which the projector, through actual interpersonal interaction with the recipient of the projective identification, exerts pressure on the Other
to experience himself and behave in congruence with the omnipotent projective phantasy.

From this starting point, Bion goes on to describe the way
in which the infant paradoxically develops the capacity to
experience his own thoughts and feelings by means of an
experience with the mother wherein the mother experiences the
infant's unthinkable thoughts, and not yet tolerable feelings, as
her own. Projective identification is viewed as a process by
which the infant's thoughts that cannot be thought and feelings
that cannot be felt are elicited in the mother when the mother
is able to make herself psychologically available to be used in
this way:

> Projective identification makes it possible for him [the
> infant] to investigate his own feelings in a personality
> powerful enough to contain them. Denial of the use of
> this mechanism, either by the refusal of the mother to
> serve as a repository for the infant's feelings, or by the
> hatred and envy of the patient who cannot allow the
> mother to exercise this function, leads to a destruction of

the link between infant and breast and consequently, to a
severe disorder of the impulse to be curious on which all
learning depends. [Bion 1959, p. 314]

Bion (1962a) used the term *reverie* to refer to the psychological state in which the (m)Other is able to successfully serve
a "containing function" for the infant's/analysand's projection
of unthought thoughts and unfelt feelings. The relationship of
container and contained is nonlinear and must not be reduced
to a linear, sequential schematization of the following sort: an
aspect of the projector in phantasy and through actual interpersonal interaction is induced in the Other; after being altered
in the process of being experienced by a "personality powerful
enough to contain them," these "metabolized" aspects of self
are made available to the projector who by means of identification becomes more fully able to experience his thoughts and
feelings as his own. Such a conception of projective identification obscures the question of the nature of the interplay of
subjectivities involved in projective identification by treating
the projector and recipient as distinct psychological entities. It
is here that the dialectical nature of Bion's concept of the
container and the contained affords the possibility of concep-
tually moving beyond the mechanical nature of the linear
understanding of projective identification just described. (See
Ogden [1979, 1982a] for clinical illustrations of the dialectical
interplay of the intrapsychic and the interpersonal dimensions
of projective identification in the analytic setting.)

From the point of view of the container/contained dialectic, projective identification becomes a conceptualization of
the creation of subjectivity through the dialectic of interpene-
tration of subjectivities. In this dialectical relationship, projector and "recipient" enter into a relationship of simultaneous
at-one-ment and separateness in which the infant's experience
is given shape by the mother, and yet (in the normative case)

the shape that the mother gives the infant has already been determined by the infant. The mother allows herself to be inhabited by the infant in her "counter-identification" (Grinberg 1962) with the infant and in this sense is created by the infant at the same time as she is creating (giving shape to) him. The shape that the mother gives to the infant is a shape that is uniquely informed by her own experience of herself and of him. (The mother's experience of this intersubjective process is only alluded to by Bion. Moreover, there is almost no discussion in Bion's work of the specific contribution of the unique psychological makeup of the mother to the mother–infant relationship.)

A mother who cannot allow herself to be inhabited and taken over from within (and thereby created) by the infant cannot give the infant psychological shape. Under these circumstances, there is "a destruction of the link between infant and breast" (Bion 1959, p. 314). The destruction of this link results in the collapse of the mutually creating intersubjectivity underlying healthy projective identification and leaves the infant without a shape with which to contain his psychological and sensory experience of himself. The terror of this experience is described by Bion as "nameless dread" (1962b, p. 116). It is nameless because it lacks the shape and definition afforded by the mother's containing/creative response to the infant's projective identifications including those provided by her conscious and unconscious symbolizing functions.

When the mother is capable of reverie, she names (gives shape to) the infant's experience through her interpretation of the infant's internal states. For instance, the infant, in the beginning, does not experience hunger; he experiences a form of physiological tension that is not yet a psychological event that can be contained by the psyche of the infant alone. The mother's act of sensing the infant's tension, her holding him, looking at him, feeding him, talking and singing to him, all represent facets of an "interpretation" of the infant's experience. In these ways, hunger is created and the infant is created as an individual (i.e., the infant's raw sensory data are transformed into a psychologically meaningful event) through the mother's recognition of his hunger.

I view the analytic process as one in which the analysand is created through an intersubjective process similar to that involved in projective identification. Analysis is not simply a method of uncovering the hidden; it is more importantly a process of creating the analytic subject who had not previously existed. For example, the analysand's history is not uncovered, it is created in the transference-countertransference and is perpetually in a state of flux as the intersubjectivity of the analytic process evolves and is interpreted by analyst and analysand (see Schafer 1976, 1978). In this way, the analytic subject is created by, and exists in an ever-evolving state in the dynamic intersubjectivity of the analytic process: the subject of psychoanalysis takes shape in the interpretive space *between* analyst and analysand. The termination of a psychoanalytic experience is not the end of the subject of psychoanalysis. The intersubjectivity of the analytic pair is appropriated by the analysand and is transformed into an internal dialogue (a process of mutual interpretation taking place within the context of a single personality system).

In light of the foregoing discussion, it can be seen that Klein's concept of projective identification, as elaborated by Bion, H. Rosenfeld, and others, presents a conceptualization of the subject interpersonally decentered from its exclusive locus within the individual; instead, the subject is conceived of as arising in a dialectic (a dialogue) of self and Other. Paradoxically, the subjectivity of the individual presupposes the existence of two subjects who together create an intersubjectivity through which the infant is created as an individual subject. The infant as subject is present from the beginning, although that subjectivity exists largely within the context of the psychological-interpersonal (containing/contained) dimension of the relationship of the infant and mother.

In summary, I have focused on three aspects of Kleinian thinking that contribute to the development of the psychoanalytic concept of the dialectically constituted/decentered subject. First, Klein's idea of "positions" represents a conception of the subject constituted in the creative and negating dialectical interplay of fundamentally different modes of generating experience. Development is no longer conceived of as a predominantly linear process involving the progression of the subject along developmental lines with pathological regressions to fixation points (see for example, Arlow and Brenner [1964]) and healthy regression (in the service of the ego [Kris 1950]). Instead, Kleinian thinking involves a temporally decentered subject generated between coexisting psychological organizations each reflecting different modes of attributing meaning to experience. The positions do not represent stages of maturity that are outgrown; instead, they represent permanent (and yet evolving) psychological organizations each providing a preserving and negating context for the others. The subject is not located in any given position, but in a space (tension) created by the dialectical interplay of the different dimensions of experience.

Second, the Kleinian conception of the splitting of ego and (internal) object extends the Freudian theme of the decentered subject by envisioning the subject as existing in a multiplicity of loci dispersed and united in psychic space. Third, the idea of projective identification (particularly, as elaborated by Bion and H. Rosenfeld) provides essential elements for a theory of the creation of the subject in the psychological space between the infant and mother (and between the analyst and analysand).

4

Winnicott's Intersubjective Subject

Winnicott's work represents a major advance in the development of the psychoanalytic conception of the subject. The implicit dialectics of Freud and Klein became the foundation of Winnicott's effort to conceptualize in analytic terms the experience of being alive as a subject. At the heart of Winnicott's (1951, 1971a) thinking is the notion that the living, experiencing subject exists neither in reality nor in fantasy, but in a potential space between the two. The Winnicottian subject is not at the beginning (and never entirely becomes) coincident with the psyche of the individual. Winnicott's conception of the creation of the subject in the space between the infant and mother involves several types of dialectical tension of unity and separateness, of internality and externality, through which the subject is simultaneously constituted and decentered from itself. I shall focus on four forms of these overlapping dialectics: (1) the dialectic of at-one-ment/separateness of mother and infant in "primary maternal preoccupation," (2) the dialectic of recognition/negation of the infant in the mirroring role of the mother, (3) the dialectic of creation/discovery of the object in transitional object relatedness, and (4) the dialectic of the creative destruction of the mother in "object usage." Each of these dialectics represents a different facet of the interdependence of subjectivity and intersubjectivity.

The Dialectic of At-One-Ment/Separateness in Primary Maternal Preoccupation

The mother–infant relationship referred to by Winnicott (1956) as "primary maternal preoccupation" involves a form of maternal identification with the infant that is so extreme that it is "almost an illness" (p. 302). The mother must "feel herself into her infant's place and so meet the infant's needs" (p. 304). In so doing, she takes the risk of losing a sense of groundedness in herself as a separate individual as well as the risk of suffering a loss of a part of herself if her infant were to die. The mother engages simultaneously in the psychological process of allowing her subjectivity to give way to that of the infant (in her experiencing his needs as her own) and at the same time maintaining sufficient sense of her own distinct subjectivity to allow herself to serve as interpreter of the infant's experience, thereby making her otherness felt, but not noticed. The intersubjectivity underlying primary maternal preoccupation involves an early form of dialectic of oneness and two-ness: the mother is an invisible presence (invisible and yet a felt presence). Through this form of relatedness, a state of "going on being" (p. 303) is generated, an apt term in that it conveys the notion of a form of subjectivity almost, but not entirely, devoid of the particularity of a sense of "I-ness." In this way, Winnicott captures something of the experience of the paradoxical simultaneity of at-one-ment and separateness.

(A related conception of intersubjectivity was suggested by Bion's [1962a] notion of the container-contained dialectic. However, Winnicott was the first to place the psychological state of the mother on an equal footing with that of the infant in the constitution of the mother–infant. This is fully articulated in Winnicott's statement, "There is no such thing as an infant [apart from the maternal provision]" [Winnicott 1960a, p. 39 fn.].)

A brief clinical example may serve to illustrate the Winnicottian dialectic under discussion in which at-one-ment is a necessary condition for twoness, and vice versa.

A rather healthy adolescent patient in the final phase of his analysis told me that he had had a dream about two tropical islands that were very close to one another. "Actually, it was just one island . . . no, there were two. I'm having a hard time explaining this . . . If you looked at the islands from above the water, there were two of them, but if you looked at them from under the water, there was really only one mass coming up from the floor of the ocean with two peaks coming out of the water that looked like, well they were, two islands. I don't know. It wasn't confusing in the dream, it just sounds confusing when I try to explain it."

I understood the two islands (that sounded very much like breasts in the patient's description) as a representation of the boy's experience of his simultaneous experience of being one "thing" with his mother (and with me in the transference) and at the same time, being distinct from her/me. The dream occurred just prior to a summer vacation break in the analysis that was serving as a symbol for the termination of the analysis. In discussing the dream, the patient came to understand the way in which it represented his feeling that he and I "could never really be apart, no matter what," and that this feeling made it possible for us to "actually be apart without losing touch with one another." In other words, oneness is the necessary context for twoness, and twoness safeguards the experience of oneness (by providing an essential negation of it). This dialectic that has its origins in the infant's experience of primary maternal preoccupation continues throughout life as a facet of all subsequent foms of subjectivity.

The "I-Me" Dialectic of the Mirroring Relationship

The experience of the infant in relation to the mirroring mother (Winnicott 1967) generates a second form of dialectical tension necessary for the creation of the subject in the space between mother and infant. "What does the baby see when he or she looks at the mother's face? I am suggesting that, ordinarily, what the baby sees is himself or herself. In other words, the mother is looking at the baby and *what she looks like is related to what she sees there*" (Winnicott 1967, p. 112).

As in the case of primary maternal preoccupation, Winnicott's description of the mother's mirroring role at first seems to represent a study in sameness, that is, a description of the way in which the mother disappears as a separate object and simply serves as a narcissistic extension of the infant. However, on closer examination, Winnicott's conception of the mirror-relationship of mother and infant is far more complex than that. Winnicott states that what the mother looks like to the infant "*is related to*," not the same as, what the mother sees in the infant. Mirroring, then, is not a relationship of identity; it is a relationship of relative sameness and therefore of relative difference. In her mirroring role, the mother (through her recognition of and identification with the infant's internal state) allows the infant to see himself as an Other (that is, to see himself at a distance from his observing, experiencing self).

Through the experience of seeing himself outside of himself (in the mirroring [m]Other), this facet of the infant's awareness of difference is not predominantly an awareness of the difference between me and not-me (i.e., the difference between self and object), but an experiencing of the difference between I and me (i.e., the difference betwen self-as-subject and self-as-object). The infant's observations of himself (as Other to himself) in the mother's reflection of him generates the rudiments of the experience of self-consciousness ("self-reflection"), that is, the awareness of observable me-ness. In other words, the mother, in her role as mirror, provides thirdness (Green 1975) that allows for the division of the infant into an observing subject and a subject-as-object with a reflective space between the two.

The experience of I-as-subject cannot exist except insofar as "I" also exist as, but am different from, me (I-as-object). The existence of I-as-subject requires the existence of me (I-as-object), otherwise, one's existence is without shape. Similarly, the self-as-object (me) presupposes the observing I-as-subject that recognizes me.

Thus, "I" and "me" have no meaning except in relation to one another: each form of experience of subjectivity creates the other and is fully dependent on the other. Moreover, "I" and "me" cannot be created by an infant in isolation from the mother. The infant requires the mirroring relationship with the mother in order to see himself as other to himself. In this way a reflective space between the poles of the dialectic of "I" and "me" is created in which the experiencing self-reflective subject is simultaneously constituted and decentered from itself.

Transitional Object Relatedness: The Dialectic of the Creation/Discovery of the Object

Perhaps the most important of Winnicott's contributions to the psychoanalytic conceptualization of the subject is his concept of transitional object relatedness (1951, 1971a). Here, Winnicott describes a form of object relationship in which the object is experienced simultaneously as created by the infant and discovered by him; the question as to which is the case simply never arises. The transitional object is an extension of the infant's internal world and at the same time has a palpable, inescapable, immutable existence outside of, and independent of, the infant. It is simultaneously a subjective object (an omnipotent creation of the infant) and the infant's "first 'not-me' possession" (Winnicott 1951, p. 1): "The essential feature . . . is *the paradox and the acceptance of the paradox*: the baby creates the object, but the object was there waiting to be created" (Winnicott 1968, p. 89). "[The paradox must not be] solved by a restatement that by its cleverness seems to eliminate the paradox" (Winnicott 1963, p. 181).

Transitional phenomena are created in the space between mother and infant, a space "that exists (but cannot exist) between the baby and the object" (Winnicott 1971b, p. 107), a space that connects and separates. The form of mother–infant relatedness in which experience of this sort is generated is a relationship that evolves from the types of intersubjectivity involved in primary maternal preoccupation and the mirroring relationship of mother and infant. The latter two forms of dialectic of oneness and separateness are more primitive in nature than transitional relatedness in that the externality of the mother is not as fully developed in them. The transitional object *is always part of the real* (as opposed to the purely psychical). It would be a contradiction in terms to speak of the "internalization" of a transitional object. An internalized object is an idea, a mental representation, and has lost its physical connection with the world outside of the infant's mind; an idea lacks actual sensory qualities, for example, of hardness, warmth, texture, and so on. Transitional object relatedness represents the first full confrontation of the infant with the irreducible alterity of the realness of the world outside of himself; and yet, paradoxically, this "full" confrontation with the real is made possible because the transitional object never ceases to be the creation of the infant, a reflection of himself in the world. "In the rules of the game we all know that we will never challenge the baby to elicit an answer to the question: did you create that or did you find it?" (Winnicott 1968, p. 89).

By means of the dialectical tension of internality and externality involved in transitional object relatedness, a third area of experiencing is generated that lies between me and not-me, between reality and fantasy, while fully partaking of both poles of these dialectics. It is in the space created between these poles that symbols are created and imaginative psychological activity takes place.

In the absence of the role played by the mother, it would be impossible for the infant to generate the conditions necessary for his coming to life as a subject in the sense addressed by the concept of the creation of transitional phenomena. The infant requires the experience of a particular form of intersubjectivity in which the mother's *being* is experienced simultaneously as an extension of himself and as other to himself. Only later is this intersubjectivity appropriated by the infant as he develops the capacity to be alone (Winnicott 1958a), that is, the capacity to be a subject independent of the actual participation of the mother's subjectivity.

The Dialectic of the Creative Destruction of the Object

The final form of the dialectic of internality and externality that I shall discuss in Winnicott's work is that of the creative destruction of the mother in the process of the development of the infant's capacity to "use" (Winnicott 1968) the mother as an external object and to feel concern for her as a subject (Winnicott 1954, 1958b). The experience of "ruth" (concern) and the capacity for object usage are interrelated achievements in that both involve forms of recognition of the alterity of the object that is related to, but different from, that involved in transitional object relatedness. In the latter, the full externality of the mother-as-object is confronted, while in the experience of "ruth" (Winnicott 1954, 1958b) (and object "usage"), it is the mother-as-subject that is fully confronted for the first time. When the object becomes a subject, the recognition of oneself by the Other creates the conditions for a new way of being aware of one's own subjectivity, and subjectivity itself is thereby altered. In other words, the experience of the recognition of one's own "I-ness" by an Other (who is recognized as an experiencing "I") creates an intersubjective dialectic through which one becomes aware of one's own subjectivity in a new way, that is, one becomes "self-conscious" (Hegel 1807) in a way that the individual had not previously experienced.

Winnicott's (1958b, 1968) understanding of the development of this aspect of subjectivity is rooted in his view of the psychological-interpersonal processes that mediate the infant's escape from the confines of the solipsism of his own omnipotent thinking and object relatedness. There is a quality of the infant's earliest relationship to the mother that Winnicott describes as "ruthless" (1958b, p. 22), that is, without ruth. The mother who is treated ruthlessly is a "subjective object," an externalization of an omnipotent internal object mother who is inexhaustible and indestructible ("a bundle of projections" [Winnicott 1968, p. 88]). Because of the mother's fantasied inexhaustibility and indestructibility there is no need for ruth; in fact, the feeling of concern does not exist in the emotional vocabulary of the infant living in a world of omnipotent object relations. (One can highly value objects, but one can feel concern only for subjects.)

Paradoxically, the process of recognition of the mother as a person for whom the infant feels concern (and a person he can "use" because of his recognition of her groundedness in the world outside of himself) involves the destruction of the mother by the infant while the mother survives (Winnicott 1954, 1968). My understanding of this paradoxical notion (which I hope is not a resolution of the paradox of the creative destruction of the mother) is that the infant makes room for the possibility of the mother as a subject, a *person* other-to-himself, by destroying an aspect of himself (his own omnipotence as projected onto the omnipotent internal object mother).

As long as the infant holds onto his defensive omnipotence in the form of his relatedness to the omnipotent internal object mother, the mother, both as a subject and as an external object, is eclipsed by the infant's projections of his omnipotent self and internal objects. The fantasied destruction of the (internal) object mother is a reflection of the infant's relinquishing of his reliance on omnipotent defenses in the form of dependence on the omnipotent internal object mother. The loosening of this tie to the omnipotent mother is an ongoing psychological task: " 'I am all the time destroying you [the mother] in (unconscious) *fantasy*' " (Winnicott 1968, p. 90). By continually (in fantasy) destroying the internal object mother, the infant becomes capable of discovering the external object mother (both as object and as subject) if the mother is able to survive the infant's fantasied destruction of her (and his ruthless treatment of her) by remaining emotionally present over time.

The very fact of the infant's fantasied destruction of the omnipotent internal object mother reflects his readiness to move beyond the solipsism of his own omnipotence and to take the risks involved in the as yet unknown experience of relatedness to objects that he has not created and that he does not own, objects that have an internal life of their own. The infant has experienced something of the otherness of the object in his relationships with transitional objects, but he has not yet fully recognized the "I-ness" of the object. As importantly, his own sense of I-ness has not yet been recognized by an Other who is also a subject.

For Winnicott, this psychological-interpersonal shift is mediated by forms of mother–infant relatedness in which the infant is experiencing the full intensity of omnipotent fantasies of destruction of the mother while the mother (as living subject) not only survives over time, but is there to catch the infant when he takes the risk of falling out of the arms of the omnipotent internal object mother into the arms of an only dimly perceived mother-in-the-world (Ogden 1985). Moreover, the mother-in-the-world is a subject who recognizes the infant's concern for her as well as the beginnings of his capacity to feel guilt about his ruthless treatment of her. The mother's subjectivity and her recognition of the subjectivity of the infant are reflected in her recognition of the infant's reparative gift (e.g., a bowel movement) after a ruthless feed (Winnicott 1954) and her acceptance of it.

In this creatively destructive process, the I-as-subject and mother-as-subject simultaneously come into being in relation to one another. (Buber [1970] uses the term *I-Thou* to refer to the relationship between oneself as subject and the Other who is experienced as being alive as a separate subject and who recognizes oneself as a subject.) A new type of intersubjective experience (a form of self-conscious subjectivity) is generated through the I-Thou dialectic, a dialectic of subjects creating one another through their recognition of one another as subjects. This conception of the space between I-as-subject and Other-as-subject represents still another way of describing the Winnicottian notion of the locus of subjectivity, a subjectivity that is always decentered from itself and is always to some degree arising in the context of intersubjectivity. In this last instance, the emphasis is on the way in which it is necessary for the omnipotence of the infant (as well as that of the adult) to be continually negated, superseded ("destroyed" in unconsciously fantasied object relations), in the process of creating a more fully generative dialectic of self and Other. In this process, subjectivity becomes aware of itself. I as self-conscious subject am created through the process of recognizing and being recognized by the Other-as-subject.

In summary, the forms of mother–infant relatedness that have been described all reflect a central theme that underlies the Winnicottian conception of the creation of the subject: the subjectivity of the infant takes shape in the potential space between mother and infant. This space is defined by a series of paradoxes that must be maintained and not resolved, paradoxes of simultaneous internality and externality, paradoxes that generate a third area of experiencing, "the place where we live" (Winnicott 1971b). Winnicott's use of the notion of paradox to describe the space in which subjectivity is created represents a quiet revolution in analytic thinking in that for the first time, a dialectical conception of the intersubjective constitution of the decentered human subject is fully articulated.

Concluding Comments

The analytic conception of the subject represents a cornerstone of the psychoanalytic project and is at the same time one of the least well-articulated psychoanalytic concepts. In Chapter 2, I discussed the way in which the concept of the psychoanalytic subject involves a conception of experiencing "I-ness" in which consciousness and unconsciousness coexist in a continual process of creative negation of one another. Consciousness and unconsciousness stand in a relationship of relative difference. The unconscious represents an order of experience that is continuous with consciousness in the sense that it participates in the same system of meanings, but differs from consciousness in the way that meanings are represented, transformed, interrelated, and so on.

Central among the contributions of psychoanalysis to a theory of subjectivity is the formulation of a concept of the subject in which neither consciousness nor unconsciousness holds a privileged position in relation to the other. Emanating from a continuous process of dialectical negation, the subject is forever decentered from static self-equivalence. That is, the psychoanalytic subject never simply is; the subject is always *becoming* through a process of the creative negation of itself.

The analytic conception of the subject has increasingly become a theory of the interdependence of subjectivity and intersubjectivity. The subject cannot create itself; the development of subjectivity requires experiences of specific forms of intersubjectivity. In the beginning, subjectivity and the individual psyche are not coincident: "There is no such thing as an infant." The constitution of the subject in the space between mother and infant is mediated by such psychological-interpersonal events as projective identification, primary maternal preoccupation, the mirroring relationship, relatedness to transitional objects, and the experiences of object usage and ruth. The appropriation by the infant of the intersubjective space represents a critical step in the establishment of the individual's capacity to generate and maintain psychological dialectics (e.g., of consciousness and unconsciousness, of me and not me, of I and me, of I and Thou) through which he is simultaneously constituted and decentered as a subject.

5

The Analytic Third: Working with Intersubjective Clinical Facts *

And he is not likely to know what is to be done unless he lives in what is not merely the present, but the present moment of the past, unless he is conscious, not of what is dead, but of what is already living.
T. S. Eliot, "Tradition and Individual Talent," 1919

On the occassion of the celebration of the seventy-fifth anniversary of the founding of *The International Journal of Psycho-Analysis* I shall endeavor to address an aspect of what I understand to be "the present moment of the past" of psycho-analysis. It is my belief that an important facet of this present moment for psychoanalysis is the development of an analytic

---

*This chapter was written by invitation of the editors of *The International Journal of Psycho-Analysis* for inclusion in the seventy-fifth anniversary issue of the *Journal* commemorating the founding of the *International Journal* by Sigmund Freud and Ernest Jones in 1920.

conceptualization of the nature of the interplay of subjectivity
and intersubjectivity in the analytic setting and the exploration
of the implications for technique that these conceptual developments hold.

In this chapter, I shall present clinical material from two
analyses in an effort to illustrate some of the ways in which an
understanding of the interplay of subjectivity and intersubjectivity influences the practice of psychoanalysis and the way in
which clinical theory is generated. As will be discussed, I
consider the dialectical movement of subjectivity and intersubjectivity to be a central clinical fact of psychoanalysis that all
clinical analytic thinking attempts to describe in ever more
precise and generative terms.

The conception of the analytic subject as it has been
elaborated in the work of Klein and Winnicott has led to an
increasingly strong emphasis on the interdependence of subject
and object in psychoanalysis. I believe that it is fair to say that
contemporary psychoanalytic thinking is approaching a point
where one can no longer simply speak of the analyst and the
analysand as separate subjects who take one another as objects.

The idea of analyst as neutral blank screen for the patient's
projections is occupying a position of steadily diminishing
importance in current conceptions of the analytic process.
"During the past half century, psychoanalysts have changed
their views of their own method. Instead of being about the
patient's intrapsychic dynamics, it is now widely held that
interpretation should be made about *the interaction* of patient
and analyst *at an intrapsychic level*" (O'Shaughnessy 1983, p.
281).[1]

_____

1. It is beyond the scope of this discussion to offer a comprehensive review
of the literature concerning the development of an intersubjective understanding of the analytic process and the nature of the interplay of transference and countertransference. A partial listing of major contributions to

My own conception of analytic intersubjectivity places central emphasis on its dialectical nature (Ogden 1979, 1982a, 1985, 1986, 1988, 1989a). This understanding represents an elaboration and extension of Winnicott's (1960a) notion that "There is no such thing as an infant [apart from the maternal provision]" (p. 39 fn.). I believe that in an analytic context, there is no such thing as an analysand apart from the relationship with the analyst, and no such thing as an analyst apart from the relationship with the analysand. Winnicott's statement quoted above is I believe intentionally incomplete. He assumes that it will be understood that the idea that there is no such thing as an infant is playfully hyberbolic and represents one element of a larger paradoxical statement. From another perspective (from the point of view of the other "pole" of the paradox), there is obviously an infant and a mother who constitute separate physical and psychological entities. The mother–infant unity coexists in dynamic tension with the mother and infant in their separateness.

Similarly, the intersubjectivity of the analyst–analysand coexists in dynamic tension with the analyst and the analysand as separate individuals with their own thoughts, feelings, sensations, corporal reality, psychological identity, and so on.

these aspects of the analytic dialogue includes Atwood and Stolorow (1984), Balint (1968), Bion (1952, 1959, 1962a), Blechner (1992), Bollas (1987), Boyer (1961, 1983, 1992), Coltart (1986), Ferenczi (1921), Gabbard (1991), Giovacchini (1979), Green (1975), Grinberg (1962), Grotstein (1981), Heimann (1950), Hoffman (1992), Jacobs (1991), Joseph (1982), Kernberg (1976), Khan (1964), Klein (1946, 1955), Kohut (1977), Little (1951), McDougall (1978), McLaughlin (1991), Meltzer (1966), Milner (1969), Mitchell (1988), Money-Kyrle (1956), O'Shaughnessy (1983), Racker (1952, 1968), D. Rosenfeld (1992), H. Rosenfeld (1952, 1965, 1971), Sandler (1976), Scharff (1992), Searles (1979), Segal (1981), Tansey and Burke (1989), Viderman (1979), and Winnicott (1947, 1951). For recent reviews of aspects of this large body of literature on transference–countertransference, see Boyer (1993) and Etchegoyen (1991).

Neither the intersubjectivity of the mother–infant nor that of
the analyst–analysand (as separate psychological entities) exists
in pure form. The intersubjective and the individually subjective each create, negate, and preserve the other. (See Chapters
3 and 4 for a discussion of the dialetic of oneness and twoness
in early development and in the analytic relationship.) In both
the relationship of mother and infant and the relationship of
analyst and analysand, the task is not to tease apart the
elements constituting the relationship in an effort to determine
which qualities belong to each individual participating in it;
rather, from the point of view of the interdependence of
subject and object, the analytic task involves an attempt to
describe as fully as one can the specific nature of the experience of the interplay of individual subjectivity and intersubjectivity.

In this chapter, I shall attempt to trace in some detail the
vicissitudes of the experience of being simultaneously within
and outside of the intersubjectivity of the analyst–analysand,
which I will refer to as "the analytic third." This third
subjectivity, the intersubjective analytic third (Green's [1975]
"analytic object"), is a product of a unique dialectic generated
by/between the separate subjectivities of analyst and analysand
within the analytic setting.[2]

---

2. Although for convenience, I shall at times refer to the "intersubjective
analytic third" as "the analytic third," or simply, "the third," this concept
should not be confused with the oedipal/symbolic third (the Lacanian [1953]
"name of the father"). The latter concept refers to a "middle term" that stands
between symbol and symbolized, between oneself and one's immediate lived
sensory experience, thereby creating a space in which the interpreting,
self-reflective, symbolizing subject is generated. In early developmental
terms, it is the father (or the "father-in-the-mother" [Ogden 1987]) who
intercedes between the mother and infant (or more accurately, the mother-
infant) thus creating the psychological space in which the elaboration of the
depressive position and oedipal triangulation occurs.

Portions of two analyses will be presented that highlight different aspects of the dynamic interplay of subjectivities constituting the analytic third. The first fragment of an analysis focuses on the importance of the most mundane, everyday aspects of the background workings of the mind (which appear to be entirely unrelated to the patient) in the service of recognizing and addressing the transference-countertransference.

The second clinical vignette provides an opportunity to consider an instance in which the analytic third was experienced by the analyst and analysand largely through the medium of somatic delusion and other forms of bodily sensations and body-related fantasies. I shall discuss the analyst's task of using verbal symbols to speak with a voice that has lived within the intersubjective analytic third, has been changed by that experience, and is able to speak *about it* in his own voice as analyst to the analysand (who has also been a part of the experience of the third).

Clinical Illustration I: The Purloined Letter

In a recent session with Mr. L., an analysand with whom I had been working for about three years, I found myself looking at an envelope on the table next to my chair in my consulting room. For the previous weeek or ten days, I had been using the envelope to jot down phone numbers retrieved from my answering machine, ideas for classes I was teaching, errands I had to attend to, and other notes to myself. Although the envelope had been in plain view for over a week, I had not noticed until that moment in the session that there was a series of vertical lines in the lower right hand portion of the front of the envelope, markings that seemed to indicate that the letter had been part of a bulk mailing. I was taken aback by a distinct feeling of disappointment. The letter that had arrived in the envelope was from a colleague in Italy who had written to me about a matter that he felt was delicate and should be kept in strictest confidence between us.

I then looked at the stamps and for the first time noticed two further details. The stamps had not been canceled and one of the three stamps had words on it that to my surprise I could read. I saw the words "Wolfgang Amadeus Mozart" and realized after a moment's delay that the words were a name with which I was familiar and were the same in Italian as they were in English.

As I retrieved myself from this reverie, I wondered how this might be related to what was going on at that moment between myself and the patient. The effort to make this shift in psychological state felt like the uphill battle of attempting to "fight repression" that I have experienced as I have attempted to remember a dream that is slipping away on waking. In years past, I have put aside such lapses of attention and have endeavored to devote myself to making sense of what the patient was saying, since in returning from such reveries I am inevitably a bit behind the patient.

I realized I was feeling suspicious about the genuineness of the intimacy that the letter had seemed to convey. My fleeting fantasy that the letter had been part of a bulk mailing reflected a feeling that I had been duped. I felt that I had been naïve and gullible, ready to believe that I was being entrusted with a special secret. I had a number of fragmentary associations that included the image of a mail sack full of letters with stamps that had not been canceled, a spider's egg sac, *Charlotte's Web*, Charlotte's message on the cobweb, Templeton the rat, and innocent Wilbur. None of these thoughts seemed to scratch the surface of what was occurring between Mr. L. and myself: I felt as if I were simply going through the motions of countertransference analysis in a way that seemed forced.

As I listened to Mr. L., a 45-year-old director of a large nonprofit agency, I was aware that he was talking in a way that was highly characteristic of him—he sounded weary and hopeless, and yet was doggedly trudging on in his production of "free associations." He had during the entire period of the analysis been struggling mightily to escape the confines of his extreme emotional detachment from himself and from other people. I thought of Mr. L.'s description of his driving up to the house in which he lives and not being able to feel it was *his* house. When he walked inside, he was greeted by "the woman and four children who lived there," but could not feel they were *his* wife and *his* children. "It's a sense of myself not being in the picture and yet I'm there. In that second of recognition of not fitting in, it's a feeling of being separate, which is right next to feeling lonely."

I tried out in my own mind the idea that perhaps I felt duped by him and taken in by the apparent sincerity of his effort to talk to me. But this idea rang hollow to me. I was reminded of the frustration in Mr. L.'s voice as he explained to me again and again that he knew that he must be feeling something, but he did not have a clue as to what it might be.

The patient's dreams were regularly filled with images of paralyzed people, prisoners, and mutes. In a recent dream he had succeeded, after expending enormous energy, in breaking open a stone only to find hieroglyphics carved into the interior surface of the stone (like a fossil). His initial joy was extinguished by his recognition that he could not understand a single element of the meaning of the hieroglyphics. In the dream, his discovery was momentarily exciting, but ultimately an empty, painfully tantalizing experience that left him in thick despair. Even the feeling of despair was almost immediately obliterated upon awaking and became a lifeless set of dream images that he "reported" to me (as opposed to telling to me). The dream had become a sterile memory and no longer felt alive as a set of feelings.

I considered the idea that my own experience in the hour might be thought of as a form of projective identification in which I was participating in the patient's experience of the despair of being unable to discern and experience an inner life that seemed to lie behind an impenetrable barrier. This formulation made intellectual sense, but felt clichéd and emotionally lacking. I then drifted into a series of narcissistic, competitive thoughts concerning professional matters that began to take on a ruminative quality. These ruminations were unpleasantly interrupted by the realization that my car, which was in a repair shop, would have to be collected before 6:00 P.M. when the shop closed. I would have to be careful to end the last analytic hour of the day precisely at 5:50 if there were to be any chance at all of my getting to the garage before it closed. I had a vivid image in my mind of myself standing in front of the closed garage doors with the traffic roaring in back of me. I felt intense helplessness and rage (as well as some self-pity) about the way in which the owner of the garage had shut his doors precisely at 6:00 despite the fact that I had been a regular customer for years and he knew full well that I would need my car. In this fantasied experience, there was a profound, intense feeling of desolation and isolation as well as a palpable physical sensation of the hardness of the pavement, the smell of the stench of the exhaust fumes, and the grittiness of the dirty glass garage door windows.

Although I was not fully conscious of it at the time, in retrospect, I can better see that I was quite shaken by this series of feelings and images that had begun with my narcissistic/competitive ruminations and had ended with the fantasies of impersonally ending the hour of my last patient of the day and then being shut out by the owner of the garage.

As I again returned to listening in a more focused way to Mr. L., I labored to put together the things that he was currently discussing: his wife's immersion in her work and the exhaustion that both he and his wife felt at the end of the day; his brother-in-law's financial reversal and impending bankruptcy; an experience while jogging in which the patient was in a near accident with a motorcyclist who was riding recklessly. I could have taken up any one of these images as a symbol of themes that we had previously discussed, including the detachment itself that seemed to permeate all that the patient was talking about as well as the disconnection I felt both from myself and from Mr. L. However, I decided not to intervene because it felt to me that if I were to try to offer an interpretation at this point, I would only be repeating myself and saying something for the sake of reassuring myself that I had something to say.

The telephone in my office had rung earlier in the session and the answering machine had clicked twice to record a message before resuming its silent vigil. At the time of the call, I had not consciously thought about who might be calling, but at this point in the hour I checked the clock to see how much longer it would be before I could retrieve the message. I felt relieved to think of the sound of a fresh voice on the answering machine tape. It was not that I imagined finding a specific piece of good news; it was more that I yearned for a crisp, clear voice. There was a sensory component to the fantasy — I could feel a cool breeze wash across my face and enter my lungs relieving the suffocating stillness of an overheated, unventilated room. I was reminded of the fresh stamps on the envelope — clear, vibrant in their colors, unobscured by the grim, mechanical, indelible scarring of machine-made cancellation marks.

I looked again at the envelope and noticed something that I had been only subliminally aware of all along: my name and address had been typed on a manual typewriter — not a computer, not a mailing label, not even an electric typewriter. I felt almost joyous about the personal quality with which my name was being "spoken." I could almost hear the idiosyncratic irregularities of each typed letter, the inexactness of the line, the way in which each "t" was missing its upper portion above the bar. This felt to me like the accent and inflection of a human voice speaking *to me*, knowing my name.

These thoughts and feelings, as well as the sensations associated with these fantasies, brought to mind (and body) something that the patient had said to me months earlier, but had not mentioned subsequently. He had told me that he felt closest to me not when I said things that seemed right, but when I made mistakes, when I got things wrong. It had taken me these months to understand in a fuller way what he had meant when he had said this to me. At this point in the session I began to be able to describe for myself the feelings of desperateness that I had been feeling in my own and the patient's frantic search for something human and personal in our work together. I also began to feel I understood something of the panic, despair, and anger associated with the experience of colliding again and again with something that appears to be human but feels mechanical and impersonal.

I was reminded of Mr. L.'s description of his mother as "brain dead." The patient could not remember a single instance of her ever having shown evidence of feeling anger or intense feeling of any sort. She immersed herself in housework and "completely uninspired cooking." Emotional difficulties were consistently met with platitudes. For example, when the patient as a 6-year-old was each night terrified that there were creatures under his bed, Mr. L.'s mother would tell him, "There's nothing there to be afraid of." This statement became a symbol in the analysis of the discord between the accuracy of the statement on the one hand (there were in fact no creatures under his bed) and the unwillingness/inability of his mother to recognize the inner life of the patient (there was something he was frightened of that she refused to acknowledge, identify with, or even be curious about).

Mr. L.'s chain of thoughts that included the idea of feeling exhausted, his brother-in-law's impending bankruptcy, and the potentially serious or even fatal accident, now struck me as a reflection of the patient's unconscious attempts to talk to me about his inchoate feeling that the analysis was depleted, bankrupt, and dying. He was experiencing the rudiments of a feeling that he and I were not talking to one another in a way that felt alive; instead, I seemed to him unable to be other than mechanical with him just as he was unable to be human with me.

I told the patient that I thought that our time together must feel to him like a joyless obligatory exercise, something like a factory job where one punches in and out with a time card. I then said that I had the sense that he sometimes feels so hopelessly stifled in the hours with me that it must feel like being suffocated in something that appears to be air, but is actually a vacuum.

Mr. L.'s voice became louder and full in a way that I had not heard before as he said, "Yes, I sleep with the windows wide open for fear of suffocating during the night. I often wake up terrified that someone is suffocating me, as if they have put a plastic bag over my head." The patient went on to say that when he walks into my consulting room, he regularly feels that the room is too warm and that the air is disturbingly still. He said that it has never once occurred to him to ask me to either turn off the heater at the foot of the couch or to open a window, in large part because he has not been fully aware until now that he has had such feelings. He said that it's terribly discouraging to realize how little he allows himself to know about what is going on inside of him, even to the point of not knowing when a room feels too warm to him.

Mr. L. was silent for the remaining 15 minutes of the session. A silence of that length had not previously occurred in the analysis. During that silence, I did not feel pressured to talk. In fact there was considerable feeling of repose and relief in the respite from what I now viewed as the "anxious mentation" that had so often filled the hours. I became aware of the tremendous effort that Mr. L. and I regularly expended in an effort to keep the analysis from collapsing into despair; I imagined the two of us in the past frantically trying to keep a beach ball in the air, punching it from one to the other. Toward the end of the hour, I became drowsy and had to fight off sleep.

The patient began the next session by saying that he had been awakened by a dream early that morning. In the dream he was underwater and could see other people who were completely naked. He noticed that he too was naked, but he did not feel self-conscious about it. He was holding his breath and felt panicky that he would drown when he could no longer hold his breath. One of the men, who was obviously breathing underwater without difficulty, told him that it would by okay if he breathed. He very warily took a breath and found that he could breathe. The scene changed although he was still underwater. He was crying in deep sobs and was feeling profound sadness. A friend whose face he could not make out talked to him. Mr. L. said that he felt grateful to the friend for not trying to reassure him or cheer him up.

The patient said that when he awoke from the dream he felt on the verge of tears. He said he got out of bed because he just wanted to feel what he was feeling although he did not know what he was sad about. Mr. L. noticed the beginnings of his familiar attempts to change the feeling of sadness into feelings of anxiety about office business or worry about how much money he had in the bank and other matters with which he "distracts" himself.

Discussion

The foregoing account was offered not as an example of a watershed in an analysis; rather, it was presented in an effort to convey a sense of the dialectical movement of subjectivity and intersubjectivity in the analytic setting. I have attempted to describe something of the way in which my experience as analyst (including the barely perceptible and often extremely mundane background workings of my mind) are contextualized by the intersubjective experience created by analyst and analysand. No thought, feeling, or sensation can be considered to be the same as it was or will be outside of the context of the

specific (and continually shifting) intersubjectivity created by
analyst and analysand.[3]

I am well aware that the form in which I presented the
clinical material was a bit odd in that I gave almost no
information of the usual sort about Mr. L. until rather late in
the presentation. This was done in an effort to convey a sense
of the degree to which Mr. L. was at times quite absent from
my conscious thoughts and feelings. My attention was not at
all focused on Mr. L. during my periods of "reverie." (I use
Bion's term *reverie* to refer not only to those psychological states
that clearly reflect the analyst's active receptivity to the analysand, but also to a motley collection of psychological states that
seem to reflect the analyst's narcissistic self-absorption, obsessional rumination, daydreaming, sexual fantasying, and so
on.)

Turning to the details of the clinical material itself as it
unfolded, my experience of the envelope (in the context of this
analysis) began with my noticing the envelope, which, despite

3. What I have said here about the analyst's thoughts and feelings being in
every instance contextualized and therefore a.ered by the experience with
the patient might seem to lead to the conclusion that everything the analyst
thinks and feels should be considered countertransference. However, I
believe that the use of the term *countertransference* to refer to everything the
analyst thinks and feels and experiences sensorially obscures the simultaneity
of the dialectic of oneness and twoness, of individual subjectivity and
intersubjectivity, that is the foundation of the psychoanalytic relationship.
To say that everything the analyst experiences is countertransference is only
to make the self-evident statement that we are each trapped in our own
subjectivity. For the concept of countertransference to have more meaning
than this, we must continually reground the concept in the dialectic of the
analyst as a separate entity and the analyst as a creation of the analytic
intersubjectivity. Neither of these "poles" of the dialectic exists in pure form
and our task is to make increasingly full statements about the specific nature
of the relationship between the experience of subject and object, between
countertransference and transference, at any given moment.

the fact that it had been physically present for weeks, came to life at that point as a psychological event, a carrier of psychological meanings, that had not existed prior to that moment. I view these new meanings not simply as a reflection of a lifting of a repression within me; rather, I understand the event as a reflection of the fact that a new subject (the analytic third) was being generated by (between) Mr. L. and myself, which resulted in the creation of the envelope as an "analytic object" (Bion 1962a, Green 1975). When I noticed this "new object" on my table, I was drawn to it in a way that was so completely ego syntonic as to be an almost completely unself-conscious event for me. I was struck by the machine-made markings on the envelope, which again had not been there (for me) to this point. I experienced these markings for the first time in the context of a matrix of meanings having to do with disappointment about the absence of a feeling of being spoken to in a way that felt personal. The uncancelled stamps were similarly "created" and took their place in the intersubjective experience that was being elaborated. Feelings of estrangement and foreignness mounted to the point that I hardly recognized Mozart's name as a part of a common language.

A detail that requires some explanation is the series of fragmentary associations having to do with *Charlotte's Web*. Although highly personal and idiosyncratic to my own life experience, these thoughts and feelings were also being created anew within the context of the experience of the analytic third. I had consciously known that *Charlotte's Web* was very important to me, but the particular significance of the book was not only repressed, it had also not yet come into being in a way that it would exist in this hour. It was not until weeks after the meeting being described that I became aware that this book was originally (and was in the process of becoming) intimately associated with feelings of loneliness. I realized for the first time (in the following weeks) that I had read this book several times during a period of intense loneliness in my childhood and that I had thoroughly identified with Wilbur as a misfit and outcast. I view these (largely unconscious) associations to *Charlotte's Web* not as a retrieval of a memory that had been repressed, but as the creation of an experience (in and through the analytic intersubjectivity) that had not previously existed in the form that it was now taking. This conception of analytic experience is central to the current paper; the analytic experience occurs at the cusp of the past and the present and involves a "past" that is being created anew (for both analyst and analysand) by means of an experience generated between analyst and analysand (i.e., within the analytic third).

Each time my conscious attention shifted from the experience of my own reveries to what the patient was saying and how he was saying it to me and being with me, I was not returning to the same place I had left seconds or minutes earlier. I was in each instance changed by the experience of the reverie, sometimes in only an imperceptibly small way. In the course of the reverie just described, something had occurred that is in no way to be considered magical or mystical. In fact, what occurred was so ordinary, so unobtrusively mundane as to be almost unobservable as an analytic event.

When I refocused my attention on Mr. L. after the series of thoughts and feelings concerning the envelope, I was more receptive to the schizoid quality of Mr. L.'s experience and to the hollowness of both his and my own attempts to create something together that felt real. I was more keenly aware of the feeling of arbitrariness associated with his sense of his place in his family and the world as well as the feeling of emptiness associated with my own efforts at being an analyst for him.

I then became involved in a second series of self-involved thoughts and feelings (following my only partially satisfactory attempt to conceptualize my own despair and that of the patient in terms of projective identification[4]). My thoughts were interrupted by anxious fantasies and sensations concerning the closing of the garage and my need to end the last analytic hour of the day on time. My car had been in the garage the entire day, but it was only with this patient at precisely this moment that the car as analytic object was created. The fantasy involving the closing of the garage was created at that moment not by me in isolation, but through my participation in the intersubjective experience with Mr. L. Thoughts and feelings concerning the car and the garage did not occur in any of the other analytic hours in which I participated that day.

In the reverie concerning the closing of the garage and my need to end the last analytic hour of the day on time, the experience of bumping up against immovable, mechanical, inhumanness in myself and others was repeated in a variety of forms. Interwoven with the fantasies were sensations of hardness (the pavement, glass, and grit) and suffocation (the exhaust fumes). These fantasies generated a sense of anxiety and urgency within me that was increasingly difficult for me to ignore (although in the past I might well have dismissed these fantasies and sensations as having no significance to the analysis except as an interference to be overcome).

Returning to listening to Mr. L., I was still feeling quite confused about what was occurring in the hour and was sorely tempted to say something in order to dissipate my feelings of powerlessness. At this point, an event that had occurred earlier in the hour (the telephone call recorded by the answering machine) occurred for the first time as an analytic event (that

---

4. I believe that an aspect of the experience I am describing can be understood in terms of projective identification, but the way in which the idea of projective identification was utilized at the point that it arose was predominantly in the service of an intellectualizing defense.

is, as an event that held meaning within the context of the intersubjectivity that was being elaborated). The voice recorded on the answering machine tape now held a promise of being the voice of a person who knew me and would speak to me in a personal way. The physical sensations of breathing freely and suffocating were increasingly important carriers of meaning. The envelope became still a different analytic object from the one that it had been earlier in the hour; it now held meaning as a representation of an idiosyncratic, personal voice (the hand-typed address with an imperfect "t").

The cumulative effect of these experiences within the analytic third led to the transformation of something the patient had said to me months earlier about feeling closest to me when I made mistakes. The patient's statement took on new meaning, but I think it would be more accurate to say that the (remembered) statement was now a new statement for me and in this sense was being made for the first time.

I began at this point in the hour to be able to use language to describe for myself something of the experience of confronting an aspect of another person and of myself that felt frighteningly and irrevocably inhuman. A number of themes that Mr. L. had been talking about took on a coherence for me that they had not held before; the themes now seemed to me to converge on the idea that Mr. L. was experiencing me and the discourse between us as bankrupt and dying. Again, these old themes were now (for me) becoming new analytic objects that I was encountering freshly. I attempted to talk to the patient about my sense of his experience of me and the analysis as mechanical and inhuman. Before I began the intervention, I did not consciously plan to use the imagery of machines (the factory and the time clock) to convey what I had in mind. I was unconsciously drawing on the imagery of my reveries concerning the mechanical (clock-determined) ending of an analytic hour and the closing of the garage. I view my choice of imagery as a reflection of the way in which I was "speaking from" the unconscious experience of the analytic third (the unconscious intersubjectivity being created by Mr. L. and myself). At the same time, I was speaking *about* the analytic third from a position as analyst outside of it.

I went on in an equally unplanned way to tell the patient of an image of a vacuum chamber (another machine) in which something that appeared to be life-sustaining air was in fact emptiness. (I was here unconsciously drawing on the sensation-images of the fantasied experience of exhaust-filled air outside the garage and the breath of fresh air associated with the answering machine fantasy.[5]) Mr. L.'s response to my intervention involved a fullness of voice that reflected a fullness of breathing (a fuller giving and taking). His own conscious and unconscious feelings of being foreclosed from the human had been experienced in the form of images and sensations of suffocation at the hands of the killing mother/analyst (the plastic bag [breast] that prevented him from being filled with life-sustaining air).

The silence at the end of the hour was in itself a new analytic event and reflected a feeling of repose that stood in marked contrast to the image of being violently suffocated in a plastic bag or of feeling disturbingly stifled by still air in my consulting room. There were two additional aspects of my experience during this silence that held significance: the fantasy of a beach ball being frantically kept aloft by being punched between Mr. L. and myself, and my feeling of drowsiness. Although I felt quite soothed by the way in which

---

5. It was in this indirect way (i.e., in allowing myself to freely draw upon my unconscious experience with the patient in constructing my interventions) that I "told" the patient about my own experience of the analytic third. This indirect communication of the countertransference contributes in a fundamental way to the feeling of spontaneity, aliveness, and authenticity of the analytic experience.

Mr. L. and I were able to be silent together (in a combination of despair, exhaustion, and hope), there was an element in the experience of the silence (in part reflected in my somnolence) that felt like far away thunder (which I retrospectively view as warded-off anger).

I shall only briefly comment on the dream with which Mr. L. opened the next hour. I understand it as simultaneously a response to the previous hour and the beginnings of a sharper delineation of an aspect of the transference-countertransference in which Mr. L.'s fear of the effect of his anger on me and of his homosexual feelings toward me were becoming predominant anxieties. (I had had clues about this earlier on that I had been unable to use as analytic objects, e.g., the image and sensation of roaring traffic behind me in my garage fantasy.)

In the first part of the dream, the patient was underwater with other naked people including a man who told him that it would be all right to breathe despite his fear of drowning. As he breathed, he found it hard to believe he was really able to do so. In the second part of Mr. L.'s dream, he was sobbing with sadness while a man whose face he could not make out stayed with him, but did not try to cheer him up. I view the dream as in part an expression of Mr. L.'s feeling that in the previous hour the two of us had together experienced and had begun to better understand something important about his unconscious ("underwater") life and that I was not afraid of being over-whelmed (drowned) by his feelings of isolation, sadness, and futility, nor was I afraid for him. As a result, he dared to allow himself to be alive (to inhale) that which he formerly feared would suffocate him (the vacuum breast/analyst). In addition, there was a suggestion that the patient's experience did not feel entirely real to him in that in the dream he found it hard to believe he was able to do what he was doing.

In the second part of Mr. L.'s dream, he more explicitly represented his enhanced ability to feel his sadness in such a way that he felt less disconnected from himself and from me. The dream seemed to me to be in part an expression of the patient's gratitude to me for not having robbed him of the feelings he was beginning to experience by interrupting the silence at the end of the previous day's meeting with an interpretation or other form of effort to dissipate or even transform his sadness with my words and ideas.

I felt that in addition to the gratitude (mixed with doubt) that Mr. L. was experiencing in connection with these events, there were less-acknowledged feelings of ambivalence toward me. I was alerted to this possibility in part by my own drowsiness at the end of the previous hour, which often reflects my own state of defendedness. The fantasy of punching the beach ball (breast) suggested that it might well be anger that was being warded off. Subsequent events in the analysis led me to feel increasingly convinced that the facelessness of the man in the second part of the dream was in part an expression of the patient's (maternal transference) anger at me for being so elusive as to be shapeless and nondescript (as he felt himself to be). This idea was borne out in the succeeding years of analysis as Mr. L.'s anger at me for "being nobody in particular" was directly expressed. In addition, on a more deeply unconscious level, the patient's being invited by the naked man to breathe in the water reflected what I felt to be an intensification of Mr. L.'s unconscious feeling that I was seducing him into being alive in the room with me in a way that often stirred homosexual anxiety (represented by the naked man's encouraging Mr. L. to take the shared fluid into his mouth). The sexual anxiety reflected in the dream was not interpreted until much later in the analysis.

Some Additional Comments

In the clinical sequence described, it was not simply fortuitous that my mind wandered and came to focus on a machine-made

set of markings on an envelope covered by scribblings of
telephone numbers, notes for teaching, and reminders to
myself about errands that needed to be done. The envelope
itself (in addition to carrying the meanings mentioned above)
also represented (what had been) my own private discourse, a
private conversation not meant for anyone else. On it were
notes in which I was talking to myself about the details of my
life. The workings of the analyst's mind during analytic hours
in these unself-conscious, natural ways are highly personal,
private, and embarrassingly mundane aspects of life that are
rarely discussed with colleagues, much less written about in
published accounts of analysis. It requires great effort to seize
this aspect of the personal and the everyday from its unself-
reflective area of reverie for the purpose of talking to ourselves
about the way in which this aspect of experience has been
transformed in such a way that it has become a manifestation
of the interplay of analytic subjects. The "personal" (the
individually subjective) is never again simply what it had been
prior to its creation in the intersubjective analytic third, nor is
it entirely different from what it had been.

I believe that a major dimension of the analyst's psychological life in the consulting room with the patient takes the
form of reverie concerning the ordinary, everyday details of
his own life (that are often of great narcissistic importance to
him). I have attempted to demonstrate in this clinical discussion that these reveries are not simply reflections of inatten-
tiveness, narcissistic self-involvement, unresolved emotional
conflict, and the like. Rather, this psychological activity
represents symbolic and protosymbolic (sensation-based)
forms given to the unarticulated (and often not yet felt)
experience of the analysand as they are taking form in the
intersubjectivity of the analytic pair (i.e., in the analytic third).

This form of psychological activity is often viewed as
something that the analyst must get through, put aside, overcome, and so forth, in his effort to be emotionally present with

and attentive to the analysand. I am suggesting that a view of the analyst's experience that dismisses this category of clinical fact leads the analyst to diminish (or ignore) the significance of a great deal (in some instances, the majority) of his experience with the analysand. I feel that a principal factor contributing to the undervaluation of such a large portion of the analytic experience is the fact that such acknowledgment involves a disturbing form of self-consciousness. The analysis of this aspect of the transference-countertransference requires an examination of the way we talk to ourselves and what we talk to ourselves about in a private, relatively undefended psychological state. In this state, the dialectical interplay of consciousness and unconsciousness has been altered in ways that resemble a dream state. In becoming self-conscious in this way, we are tampering with an essential inner sanctuary of privacy and therefore with one of the cornerstones of our sanity. We are treading on sacred ground, an area of personal isolation in which, to a large extent, we are communicating with subjective objects (Winnicott 1963; see also Chapter 9). This communication (like the notes to myself on the envelope) are not meant for anyone else, not even for aspects of ourselves that lie outside of this exquisitely private/mundane "cul-de-sac" (Winnicott 1963, p. 184). This realm of transference-countertransference experience is so personal, so ingrained in the character structure of the analyst that it requires great psychological effort to enter into a discourse with ourselves in a way that is required to recognize that even this aspect of the personal has been altered by our experience in and of the analytic third. If we are to be analysts in a full sense, we must self-consciously attempt to bring even this aspect of ourselves to bear on the analytic process.

The Psyche-Soma and the Analytic Third

In the following section of this chapter, I present an account of an analytic interaction in which a somatic delusion experienced by the analyst, and a related group of bodily sensations and body-related fantasies experienced by the analysand, constituted a principal medium through which the analytic third was experienced, understood, and interpreted. As will become evident, the conduct of this phase of the analysis depended on the analyst's capacity to recognize and make use of a form of intersubjective clinical fact manifested in large part through bodily sensation/fantasy.

Clinical Illustration II: The Tell-Tale Heart

In this clinical discussion, I shall describe a series of events that occurred in the third year of the analysis of Mrs. B., a 42-year-old married attorney and mother of two latency-aged children. The patient had begun analysis for reasons that were not clear to either of us. Mrs. B. had felt vaguely discontented with her life despite the fact that she had "a wonderful family" and was doing well in her work. She told me that she never would have guessed that she would have "ended up in an analyst's office." "It feels like I've stepped out of a Woody Allen film."

The first year-and-a-half of analysis had a labored and vaguely unsettling feeling to it. I was puzzled by why Mrs. B. was coming to her daily meetings and was a bit surprised each day when she appeared. The patient almost never missed a session, was rarely late, and in fact, arrived early enough to use the lavatory in my office suite prior to almost every meeting.

Mrs. B. spoke in an organized, somewhat obsessional, but thoughtful way; there were always "important" themes to discuss including her mother's jealousy of even small amounts of attention paid to the patient by her father. Mrs. B. felt that this was connected with current difficulties such as her inability to learn ("take things in") from female senior partners at work. Nonetheless, there was a superficiality to this work and as time went on it seemed to require greater and greater effort for the patient to "find things to talk about." The patient talked about not feeling fully present in the meetings despite her best efforts to "be here."

Toward the end of the second year of analysis, the silences had become increasingly frequent and considerably longer in duration, often lasting 15 to 20 minutes. (In the first year, there had rarely been a silence.) I attempted to talk with Mrs. B. about what it felt like for her to be with me in a given period of silence. She would say that she felt extremely frustrated and stuck, but was unable to elaborate. I offered my own tentative thoughts about the possible relationship between a given silence and the transference-countertransference experience that had immediately preceded the silence or had been left unresolved in the previous meeting. None of these interventions seemed to alter the situation.

Mrs. B. repeatedly apologized for not having more to say and worried that she was failing me. As months passed, there was a growing feeling of exhaustion and despair associated with the silences and with the overall lifelessness of the analysis. The patient's apologies to me for this state of affairs continued, but became increasingly unspoken and were conveyed by her facial expression, gait, tone of voice, and so on. Also, at this juncture in the analysis, Mrs. B. began to wring her hands throughout the analytic hours, but more vigorously during the silences. She pulled strenuously on the fingers of her hands and deeply kneaded her knuckles and fingers to the point that her hands became reddened in the course of the hour.

I found that my own fantasies and daydreams were unusually sparse during this period of work. I also noticed that I experienced less of a feeling of closeness to Mrs. B. than I would have expected. One morning while driving to my office, I was thinking of the people I would be seeing that day and could not remember Mrs. B.'s first name. I rationalized that I recorded only her last name in my appointment book and never addressed her by her first name, nor did she ever mention her first name in talking about herself as many patients do. I imagined myself to be a mother unable to give her baby a name after its birth as a result of profound ambivalence on the part of the mother concerning the birth of the baby. Mrs. B. had told me very little about her parents and her childhood. She said that it was terribly important to her that she tell me about her parents in a way that was both "fair and accurate." She said that she would tell me about them when she found the right way and the right words to do so.

During this period I developed what I felt to be a mild case of the flu, but was able to keep my appointments with all of my patients. In the weeks that followed, I noticed that I continued not to feel physically well during my meetings with Mrs. B., and experienced feelings of malaise, nausea, and vertigo. I felt like a very old man and, for reasons I could not understand, I took some comfort in this image of myself while at the same time deeply resenting it. I was not aware of similar feelings and physical sensations during any other parts of the day. I concluded that this reflected a combination of the fact that the meetings with Mrs. B. must have been particularly draining for me and that the long periods of silence in her meetings allowed me to be more conscious of my physical state than I was with other patients.

In retrospect, I am able to recognize that in this period of work I began to feel diffuse anxiety during the hours with Mrs. B. However, at the time I was only subliminally aware of this anxiety and was hardly able to differentiate it from the physical sensations I was experiencing. Just before my meetings with Mrs. B., I would regularly find things to do such as making phone calls, sorting papers, finding a book, and so on, all of which had the effect of delaying the moment when I would have to meet the patient in the waiting room. As a result, I was occasionally a minute or so late in beginning the hours.

Mrs. B. seemed to look at me intently at the beginning and end of each hour. When I asked her about it, she apologized and said that she was not aware of doing so. The content of Mrs. B.'s associations had a sterile, highly controlled feeling to it and centered on difficulties at work and worries about possible emotional troubles that she felt her children were having. She brought her older child for a consultation with a child psychiatrist because of her worry that he could not concentrate well enough in school. I commented that I thought Mrs. B. was worried about her own value as a mother just as she was worried about her value as a patient. (This interpretation was partially correct, but failed to address the central anxiety of the hour because, as will be discussed, I was unconsciously defending against recognizing it.)

Not long after I made the intervention concerning the patient's self-doubts concerning her value as a mother and analysand, I felt thirsty and leaned over in my chair to take a sip from a glass of water that I keep on the floor next to my chair. (I had on many occasions done the same thing during Mrs. B.'s hours and during the hours of other patients.) Just as I was reaching for the glass, Mrs. B. startled me by abruptly (and for the first time in the analysis) turning around on the couch to look at me. The patient had a look of panic on her face and said, "I'm sorry, I didn't know what was happening to you."

It was only in the intensity of this moment in which there was a feeling of terror that something catastrophic was happening to me that I became able to name for myself the terror that I had been carrying for some time. I became aware that the anxiety I had been feeling and the (predominantly unconscious and primitively symbolized) dread of the meetings with Mrs. B. (that was reflected in my procrastinating behavior) had been directly connected with an unconscious sensation/fantasy that my somatic symptoms of malaise, nausea, and vertigo were caused by Mrs. B. and that she was killing me. I now understood that I had for several weeks been emotionally consumed by the unconscious conviction (a "fantasy in the body," [Gaddini 1982, p. 143]) that I had a serious illness, perhaps a brain tumor, and during that period had been frightened that I was dying. I felt an immense sense of relief at this point in the meeting as I came to understand these thoughts, feelings, and sensations as reflections of transference-countertransference events occuring in the analysis.

I said to Mrs. B. in response to her turning to me in fright that I thought she had been afraid that something terrible was happening to me and that I might even be dying. She said that she knew it sounded crazy, but when she heard me moving in my chair she became filled with the feeling that I was having a heart attack. She added that she had felt that I had looked ashen for some time, but she had not wanted to insult me or worry me by saying so. (Mrs. B.'s capacity to speak to me about her perceptions, feelings, and fantasies in this way reflected the fact that a significant psychological shift had already begun to take place.)

I realized as this was occuring that it was I who Mrs. B. had wanted to take to see a doctor, not her older child. I recognized that the interpretation that I had given earlier in the hour about her self-doubt had been considerably off the mark and that the anxiety about which the patient was trying to tell me was her fear that something catastrophic was occurring between us (that would kill one or both of us) and that a third person (an absent father) must be found in order to prevent the disaster from occurring. I had often moved in my chair during Mrs. B.'s hours, but it was only at the moment described that the noise of my movement in my chair became an "analytic object" (a carrier of intersubjectively generated analytic meaning) that had not previously existed. My own and the patient's capacity to think as separate individuals had been co-opted by the intensity of the shared unconsious fantasy/somatic delusion in which we were both enmeshed. The unconscious fantasy reflected an important, highly conflicted set of Mrs. B.'s unconscious internal object relationships that were being created anew in the analysis in the form of my somatic delusion in conjunction with the patient's delusional fears (about my body) and her own sensory experiences (e.g., her handwringing).

I told Mrs. B. that I felt that not only was she afraid that I was dying, I thought she was also afraid that she was the direct and immediate cause of it. I said that just as she had worried that she was having a damaging effect on her son and had taken him to a doctor, she was afraid that she was making me so ill that I would die. At this

point, Mrs. B.'s handwringing and finger-tugging sub-
sided. I realized then, as Mrs. B. began to use hand
movements as an accompaniment to her verbal expression, that I could not recall ever having seen her hands
operate separately (i.e., neither touching one another,
nor moving in a rigid, awkward way). The patient said
that what we were talking about felt true to her in an
important way, but she was worried that she would forget
everything that had occurred in our meeting that day.

Mrs. B.'s last comment reminded me of my own
inability to remember her first name and my fantasy of
being a mother unwilling to fully acknowledge the birth
of her baby (by not giving it a name). I now felt that the
ambivalence represented by my own act of forgetting and
the associated fantasy (as well as Mrs. B.'s ambivalence
represented in her anxiety that she would obliterate all
memory of this meeting) reflected a fear jointly held by
Mrs. B. and myself that allowing her "to be born" (i.e., to
become genuinely alive and present) in the analysis would
pose a serious danger to both of us. I felt that we had
created an unconscious fantasy (largely generated in the
form of bodily experience) that her coming to life (her
birth) in the analysis would make me ill and could
possibly kill me. For both our sakes, it was important that
we make every effort to prevent that birth (and death)
from occurring.

I said to Mrs. B. that I thought I understood a little
better now why she felt that despite every effort on her
part, she could not feel present here with me and had
increasingly not been able to think of anything to say. I
told her that I thought she was attempting to be invisible
in her silence as if she were not actually here and that she
hoped that in doing so she would be less of a strain on me
and keep me from becoming ill.

She responded that she was aware that she apologized to me continually and that at one point she felt so fed up with herself that she felt, but did not say to me, that she was sorry that she ever "got into this thing" (the analysis) and wished she could "erase it, make it never have happened." She added that she thought that I would be better off, too, and she imagined that I was sorry that I had ever agreed to work with her. She said that this was similar to a feeling that she had had for as long as she could remember. Although her mother repeatedly assured her that she had been thrilled to be pregnant with the patient and had looked forward to her birth, Mrs. B. felt convinced that she had "been a mistake" and that her mother had not wanted to have children at all. Her mother was in her late thirties and her father in his mid-forties when the patient was born. Mrs. B. was an only child and as far as the patient knew, there were no other pregnancies. Mrs. B. told me that her parents were very "devoted" people and so she feels extremely unappreciative for saying so, but her parents' home did not feel to her to be a place for children. Her mother kept all the toys in the patient's room so that her father, a "serious academic," would not be disturbed as he read and listened to music in the evenings and on weekend afternoons.

Mrs. B.'s behavior in the analysis seemed to reflect an immense effort to behave "like an adult" and not to make an emotional mess of "my home" (the analysis) by strewing it with irrational or infantile thoughts, feelings, or behavior. I was reminded of her comments in the opening meeting about the foreignness and sense of unrealness that she felt in my office (feeling that she had stepped out of a Woody Allen film). Mrs. B. had unconsciously been torn by her need for help from me and her fear that the very act of claiming a place for herself with me (in me) would deplete or kill me. I was able to understand my fantasy (and associated sensory experiences) of having a brain tumor as a reflection of an unconscious fantasy that the patient's very existence was a kind of growth that greedily, selfishlessly, and destructively took up space that it had no business occupying.

Having told me about her feelings about her parents' home, Mrs. B. reiterated her concern that she would present an inaccurate picture of her parents (particularly her mother) leading me to see her mother in a way that did not accurately reflect the totality of who she was. However, the patient added that saying this felt more reflexive than real this time.

During these exchanges, I felt for the first time in the analysis that there were two people in the room talking to one another. It seemed to me that not only was Mrs. B. able to think and talk more fully as a living human being, but that I also felt that I was thinking, feeling, and experiencing sensations in a way that had a quality of realness and spontaneity of which I had not previously been capable in this analysis. In retrospect, my analytic work with Mrs. B. to this point had sometimes felt to me to involve an excessively dutiful identification with my own analyst (the "old man"). I had not only used phrases that he had regularly used, but also at times spoke with an intonation that I associated with him. It was only after the shift in the analysis just described that I fully recognized this. My experience in the phase of analytic work being discussed had "compelled me" to experience the unconscious fantasy that the full realization of myself as an analyst could occur only at the cost of the death of another part of myself (the death of an internal object analyst/father). The feelings of comfort, resentment, and anxiety associated with my fantasy of being an old man reflected both the safety that I felt in being like (with) my analyst/father and the wish to be free of him (in fantasy, to kill him). The latter wish carried with it the fear that I would die in the process. The experience with Mrs. B., including the act of putting my thoughts, feelings, and sensations into words, constituted a particular form of separation and of mourning of which I had not been capable to that point.

Concluding Comments on the Concept of the Analytic Third

In closing, I will attempt to bring together a number of ideas about the notion of the analytic third that have been either explicitly or implicitly developed in the course of the two foregoing clinical discussions.

The analytic process reflects the interplay of three subjectivities: the subjectivity of the analyst, of the analysand, and of the analytic third. The analytic third is a creation of the analyst and analysand, and at the same time the analyst and analysand (*qua* analyst and analysand) are created by the analytic third. (There is no analyst, no analysand, no analysis in the absence of the third.)

Because the analytic third is experienced by analyst and analysand in the context of his or her own personality system, personal history, psychosomatic makeup, and so on, the experience of the third (although jointly created) is not identical for each participant. Moreover, the analytic third is an asymmetrical construction because it is generated in the context of the analytic setting, which is powerfully defined by the relationship of roles of analyst and analysand. As a result, the unconscious experience of the analysand is privileged in a

specific way, that is, it is the past and present experience of the
analysand that is taken by the analytic pair as the principal
(although not exclusive) subject of the analytic discourse. The
analyst's experience in and of the analytic third is (primarily)
utilized as a vehicle for the understanding of the conscious and
unconscious experience of the analysand. (Analyst and analysand are not engaged in a democratic process of mutual
analysis.)

The concept of the analytic third provides a framework of
ideas about the interdependence of subject and object, of
transference and countertransference, that assists the analyst
in his efforts to attend closely to, and think clearly about, the
myriad of intersubjective clinical facts encountered by the
analyst, whether they be the apparently self-absorbed ram-
blings of his mind, the analyst's bodily sensations that seemingly have nothing to do with the analysand, or any other
"analytic object" intersubjectively generated by the analytic
pair.

Summary

In this chapter, two clinical sequences are presented in an
effort to describe the methods by which the analyst attempts to
recognize, understand, and verbally symbolize for himself and
the analysand the specific nature of the moment-to-moment
interplay of the analyst's subjective experience, the subjective
experience of the analysand, and the intersubjectively generated experience of the analytic pair (the experience of the
analytic third).

In the first clinical discussion, I describe how the intersubjective experience created by the analytic pair becomes
accessible to the analyst in part through the analyst's experience of his own reveries, forms of mental activity that often

appear to be nothing more than narcissistic self-absorption, distractedness, compulsive rumination, daydreaming, and the like. The second clinical account focuses on an instance in which the analyst's somatic delusion, in conjunction with the analysand's sensory experiences and body-related fantasies, served as a principal medium through which the analyst experienced and came to understand the meaning of the leading anxieties that were being (intersubjectively) generated.

6

Projective Identification and the Subjugating Third

> *We are still in the process of discovering what*
> *projective identification "means," not that Mrs. Klein*
> *meant all that in 1946, consciously or otherwise.*
> Donald Meltzer, 1978, p. 39

In this chapter, I shall offer some reflections on the process of projective identification as a form of intersubjective thirdness. In particular, I shall describe the interplay of mutual subjugation and mutual recognition that I view as fundamental to this psychological-interpersonal event.

In Klein's (1946, 1955) work, projective identification was only implicitly a psychological-interpersonal concept. However, the concept as it has been developed by Bion (1952, 1962a) and H. Rosenfeld (1952, 1971, 1987), and further enriched by Grotstein (1981), Joseph (1987), Kernberg (1987), Meltzer (1966), Ogden (1979), O'Shaughnessy (1983), Segal (1981), and others, has taken on an increasingly complex set of

intersubjective meanings and clinical applications. The understanding of projective identification that I shall propose is
founded on a conception of psychoanalysis as a process in
which a variety of forms of intersubjective "thirdness" are
generated that stand in dialectical tension with the analyst and
analysand as separate psychological entities. In projective
identification, a distinctive form of analytic thirdness is generated in the dialectic of subjectivity and intersubjectivity that
I shall refer to as "the subjugating third," since this form of
intersubjectivity has the effect of subsuming within it (to a
very large degree) the individual subjectivities of the participants.

The Concept of Projective Identification

I use the term *projective identification* to refer to a wide range of
psychological-interpersonal events, including the earliest forms
of mother–infant communication (Bion 1962a), fantasied coercive incursions into and occupation of the personality of
another person, schizophrenic confusional states (H. Rosenfeld 1952), and healthy "empathic sharing" (Pick 1985, p. 45).
(The understanding of projective identification that will be
presented has evolved in the course of a series of papers that I
have written over the past fifteen years [Ogden 1978a,b, 1979,
1980, 1981, 1982a,b, 1984, 1985, 1986, 1988, 1989a]. Detailed
descriptions of the phenomenology of projective identification
are contained in these papers as well as in Chapters 5 and 8 of
this volume.)
      Despite the breadth of psychological-interpersonal phe-
nomena addressed by the concept, I view projective identification as a discrete form (or more accurately, a quality) of
intersubjective experience. Projective identification is not an

experience that occurs in isolation from the rest of the emotional life of the individual. It is a quality of emotional life that coexists with a multiplicity of other qualities. It therefore contributes to, rather than defines; it provides colorations to a life experience rather than constituting the entirety of an experience. I view projective identification as a dimension of all intersubjectivity, at times the predominant quality of the experience, at other times only a subtle background.

Projective identification involves unconscious narratives (both verbally and nonverbally symbolized) involving the fantasy of evacuating a part of oneself into another person. This fantasied evacuation serves the purpose of either protecting oneself from the dangers posed by an aspect of oneself or of safeguarding a part of oneself by depositing it in another person who is experienced as only partially differentiated from oneself (Klein 1946, 1955; see also Chapter 3). The aspect of oneself that is in unconscious fantasy "residing" in the other person is felt to be altered in the process, and under optimal conditions is imagined to be "retrieved" in a less toxic or endangered form. Alternatively, under pathogenic conditions the reappropriated part may be felt to have been deadened or to have become more persecutory than it had previously been.

Inextricably connected with this set of unconscious fantasies is a set of interpersonal correlates to the unconscious fantasies (Bion 1959, Joseph 1987, H. Rosenfeld 1971, 1987). The interpersonal quality of the psychological event does not follow from the unconscious fantasy; the unconscious fantasy and the interpersonal event are *two aspects of a single psychological event*.

The interpersonal facet of projective identification involves a transformation of the subjectivity of the "recipient" in such a way that the separate "I-ness" of the other-as-subject is (for a time and to a degree) subverted: "You [the 'recipient' of the projective identification] are me [the projector] to the extent that I need to make use of you for the purpose of experiencing through you what I cannot experience myself. You are not me to the extent that I need to disown an aspect of myself and in fantasy hide myself (disguised as not-me) in you." The recipient of the projective identification becomes a participant in the negation of himself as a separate subject, thus making "psychological room" in himself to be (in unconscious fantasy) occupied (taken over) by the projector.

The projector in the process of projective identification has unconsciously entered into a form of negation of himself as a separate I and in so doing has become other-to-himself; he has become (in part) an unconscious being outside of himself who is simultaneously I and not I. The recipient is and is not oneself at a distance. The projector is becoming someone other than who he had been to that point. The projector's experience of occupying the recipient is an experience of negating the other as subject and co-opting his subjectivity with one's own subjectivity, while the occupying part of the projector's self is objectified (experienced as a part object) and disowned. The outcome of this mutually negating process is the creation of a third subject, "the subject of projective identification," that is both and neither projector and/nor recipient. Thus, projective identification is a process by which the subjectivity of both projector and recipient are being negated in different ways: the projector is disavowing an aspect of himself that he imagines to be evacuated into the recipient while the recipient is participating in a negation of himself by surrendering to (making room for) the disavowed aspect of the subjectivity of the projector.

It does not suffice to say that projective identification simply represents a powerful form of projection or of identification or a summation of the two since the concepts of projection and identification address only the intrapsychic dimension of experience. Rather, projective identification can be understood only in terms of a mutually creating, negating, and preserving dialectic of subjects, each of whom allows himself to be "subjugated" by the other, that is, negated in such a way as to become, through the other, a third subject (the subject of projective identification). What is distinctive about projective identification as a form of analytic relatedness is that the analytic intersubjectivity characterizing it is one in which the (asymmetrical) mutual subjugation (that mediates the process of creating a third subjectivity) has the effect of powerfully subverting the experience of analyst and analysand as separate subjects. In the analytic setting, projective identification involves a type of partial collapse of the dialectical movement of subjectivity and intersubjectivity resulting in the subjugation (of the individual subjectivities of analyst and analysand) by the analytic third. The analytic process, if successful, involves the reappropriation of the individual subjectivities of analyst and analysand, which have been transformed through their experience of (in) the newly created analytic third (the "subject of projective identification").

Projective identification can be thought of as involving a central paradox: the individuals engaged in this form of relatedness unconsciously subjugate themselves to a mutually generated intersubjective third (the subject of projective identification) for the purpose of freeing themselves from the limits of who they had been to that point.

In projective identification, analyst and analysand are each limited and enriched; each is stifled and vitalized. The new intersubjective entity that is created, the subjugating analytic third, becomes a vehicle through which thoughts might be thought, feelings might be felt, sensations might be experienced, which to that point had existed only as potential experiences for each of the individuals participating in this psychological-interpersonal process. In order for psychological growth to occur, there must be a superseding of the subju-

gating third and the establishment of a new and more generative dialectic of oneness and twoness, similarity and difference, individual subjectivity and intersubjectivity.

Although Klein (1955) focused almost entirely on the
experience of psychological depletion involved in projective
identification, it is now widely understood that projective
identification also involves the creation of something potentially larger and more generative than either of the participants
(in isolation from one another) is capable of generating. The
vitalization or expansion of the individual subject is not
exclusively an aspect of the experience of the projector; the
"recipient" of a projective identification does not simply experience the event as a form of psychological burden in which he
is limited and deadened. In part, this is due to the fact that
there is never a recipient who is not simultaneously a projector
in a projective identificatory experience. The interplay of
subjectivities is never entirely one sided; each person is being
negated by the other while being newly created in the unique
dialectical tension generated by the two.

The recipient of the projective identification is engaged
in a negation (subversion) of his own individuality in part for
the unconscious purpose of disrupting the closures underlying
the coherence/stagnation of the self. Projective identification
offers the recipient the possibility of creating a new form of
experience that is other-to-himself, and thereby creates conditions for the alteration of who he had been to that point and
who he had experienced himself to be. The recipient is not
simply identifying with an other (the projector); he is becoming an other and experiencing (what is becoming) himself
through the subjectivity of a newly created other/third/self.

The two subjects entering into a projective identification
(albeit involuntarily) each unconsciously attempts to overcome
(negate) himself and in so doing make room for the creation of

a novel subjectivity, an experience of I-ness that each individual in isolation could not have created for himself. In one sense, we participate in projective identification (often despite our most strenuous conscious efforts to avoid doing so) in order to create ourselves in and through the other-who-is-not-fully-other; at the same time, we unconsciously allow ourselves to serve as the vehicle through which the other (who is not fully other) creates himself as subject through us. In different ways, each of the individuals entering into a projective identification experiences both aspects (both forms of negating and being negated) in this intersubjective event. It does not suffice to simply say that in projective identification one finds oneself playing a role in someone else's unconscious fantasy (Bion 1959). More fully stated, one finds oneself unconsciously both playing a role in and serving as author of someone else's unconscious fantasy.

In projective identification, one unconsciously abrogates a part of one's own separate individuality in order to move beyond the confines of that individuality; one unconsciously subjugates oneself in order to free oneself from oneself. The generative freeing of the individual participants from the subjugating "third" depends upon the analyst's act of recognition of the individuality of the analysand (and of himself) (e.g., by means of the accurate and empathic understanding and interpretation of the transference–countertransference) and by the recognition of the individuality of the analyst (and analysand) by the analysand (e.g., through the analysand's use of the analyst's interpretation).

Hegel's (1807) allegory of the master and slave (particularly as discussed by Kojève [1934–1935]) provides vivid language and imagery for the understanding of the creation and negation (the superseding) of the subjugating third of projective identification. In Hegel's allegory, at the "beginning of history," in the initial encounter of two human beings, each senses that his capacity to experience his own sense of I-ness, his own self-consciousness, is somehow contained in the other.

> Self-consciousness [in a rudimentary form] is faced by another self-consciousness; it has come *out of itself*. This has a twofold significance: first, it has lost itself, for it finds itself as an *other* being; secondly, in doing so it has superseded the other, for it does not see the other as an essential being, but in the other [at first] sees [only] its own self. [Hegel 1807, p. 111]

Each individual cannot simply become a self-conscious subject by seeing himself in the other, that is, by projecting himself into the other person and experiencing the other as himself. "He must overcome his being-outside-of-himself" (Kojève 1934–1935, p. 13). Each individual is destined to remain outside of himself (alienated from himself) insofar as the other has not "'given him back' to himself by recognizing him" (p. 13). It is only through the recognition by an other who is recognized as a separate (and yet interdependent) person that one becomes increasingly (self-reflectively) human. One's being outside of oneself (for example, one's being *within* the subject of projective identification) is only a potential form of being. The act of having oneself "given back" by the other is not a returning of oneself to an original state; rather, it is a creation of oneself as a (transformed, more fully human, self-reflective) subject for the first time. An intersubjective dialectic of recognizing and being recognized serves as the foundation of the creation of individual subjectivity. If there is a failure of recognition of each by the other, "the middle term [the dialectical tension] collapses . . . in a dead unity" (p. 14) of static, non-self-reflective being: each leaves the other alone "as things" and does not participate in an interpersonal process in which each "gives the other back" to himself or herself thereby creating individual subjectivity. (It is important to note that the use of the term and concept *intersubjectivity* is not a contribution of contemporary psychology; rather, it is an idea that for centuries has been used in philosophy in the way I have just described.)

The projector and the recipient of a projective identification are unwitting, unconscious allies in the project of using the resources of their individual subjectivities and their intersubjectivity to escape the solipsism of their own separate psychological existences. They each have circled in the realm of their own internal object relations from which even the intrapsychic discourse that we call "self-analysis" can offer little in the way of lasting psychological change when isolated from intersubjective experience. (This is not to say that self-analysis is without value; rather, I believe that it has severe limitations when isolated from intersubjective spheres such as those provided by projective identification.) Human beings have a need as deep as hunger and thirst to establish intersubjective constructions (including projective identifications) in order to find an exit from unending, futile wanderings in their own internal object world. It is in part for this reason that consultation with colleagues and supervisors plays such an important role in the practice of psychoanalysis.

The unconscious intersubjective "alliance" involved in projective identification may have qualities that feel to the participants like something akin to a kidnapping, blackmailing, seduction, a mesmerization, being swept along by the irresistible frightening lure of an unfolding horror story, and so on. However, the degree of pathology associated with a given projective identificatory experience is not to be measured by the degree of coercion involved in the fantasied subjugation; rather, pathology in projective identificatory experience is a reflection of the degree of inability/unwilling-

ness of the participants to release one another from the
subjugation of the "third" by means of an act of recognition
(often mediated by means of interpretation) of the unique and
separate individuality of the other and of oneself. (Of course,
the separateness always stands in dialectical tension with
interdependence.)

Summary

In this chapter the nature of the interplay of subjectivity and
intersubjectivity that is specific to projective identification is
discussed. In projective identification, there is a partial collapse of the dialectical movement of individual subjectivity and
intersubjectivity and a resultant creation of a subjugating
analytic third (within which the individual subjectivities of the
participants are to a large degree subsumed). A successful
analytic process involves the superseding of the third and the
reappropriation of the (transformed) subjectivities by the
participants as separate (and yet interdependent) individuals.
This is achieved through an act of mutual recognition that is
often mediated by the analyst's interpretation of the transference-countertransference and the analysand's use of the
analyst's interpretation.

7

The Concept of
Interpretive Action

We say ourselves in syllables that rise
From the floor, saying ourselves in speech we do not
speak.

Wallace Stevens,
"The Creations of Sound," 1947*

At this point in the development of psychoanalytic thought, it is generally accepted that action (other than verbal symbolization) constitutes an important medium through which the analysand communicates specific unconscious meanings to the analyst, for example through the actions mediating projective identifications (Ogden 1982a, H. Rosenfeld 1971), "role responsiveness" (Sandler 1976), "evocation by proxy" (Wangh 1962), "enactments" (McLaughlin 1991), and so on. However,

---

it has been very little recognized that many of the analyst's most critical transference interpretations are conveyed to the analysand by means of the analyst's actions. It is this aspect of the analytic process, the analyst's "interpretive actions," that is the focus of this chapter.

By "interpretive action" (or "interpretation-in-action") I mean the analyst's communication of his understanding of an aspect of the transference-countertransference to the analysand by means of activity other than that of verbal symbolization.[1] At times such activity is disconnected from words (e.g., the facial expression of the analyst as a patient lingers at the consulting room door); at times the analyst's activity (as medium for interpretation) takes the form of "verbal action," for example, the setting of the fee, the announcement of the ending of the hour, or the insistence that the analysand put a stop to a given form of acting in or acting out; at times interpretive action involves the voice, but not words (e.g., the analyst's laughter).

The significance of interpretive action lies in its capacity to convey to the analysand aspects of the analyst's understanding of unconscious transference-countertransference meanings at a time when such understandings cannot be communicated to the patient in the form of verbally symbolized interpretation alone. Of course, an action in itself (in isolation from a matrix of intersubjectively generated symbols) is without meaning; interpretive actions acquire their specificity of meaning from the way in which they are generated within the context of the experience of analyst and analysand in the "intersubjective analytic third."

I am focusing in this chapter, not on the conveying of

---

1. In this chapter, the notion of interpretation will be used to refer to a "procedure [which] . . . brings out the latent meaning in what the subject says and does" (Laplanche and Pontalis 1967, p. 227).

affect or the creation of a mutative emotional "climate" (Balint 1968, p. 160) or "atmosphere" (p. 160) through the analyst's actions; rather, my focus is on the use of action as *an interpretive medium* through which the analyst conveys specific aspects of his understanding of unconscious transference-countertransference meaning. There has been considerable discussion in the analytic literature of the analyst's actions (other than verbal interpretation) as agents for therapeutic change (see for example, Alexander and French 1946, Balint 1968, Casement 1982, Coltart 1986, Ferenczi 1921, Klauber 1976, Little 1960, Mitchell 1993, H. Rosenfeld 1978, Stewart 1990, Symington 1983, and Winnicott 1947). However, the idea of the analyst's actions as a medium for the interpretation of the transference-countertransference has been very little explored. Contributions by Coltart (1986), H. Rosenfeld (1978), and Stewart (1977, 1987, 1990) have discussed the impact of the analyst's actions in ways that overlap my own conception of interpretive action. However, the emphasis in these latter papers is on the use of the analyst's actions in the service of (re)establishing conditions in which analyst and analysand might reflect on the events (often an acting out or acting in) that have been occurring in the analysis. In contrast, my own focus is on the analyst's actions as an interpretive vehicle for conveying to the patient specific aspects of the analyst's understanding of unconscious transference–countertransference meanings (which understanding is derived from the analyst's experience in and of the analytic third).

I shall attempt to frame the discussion of the concept of interpretation in action in such a way that it does not fall prey to forms of reductionism that are regularly so large a part of the discussion of the question of whether interpretation or object relationship is the greater (or exclusive) therapeutic agent in psychoanalysis. I take it for granted that interpretation is a form of object relationship and that object relationship is a form of interpretation (in the sense that every object relationship conveys an aspect of the subject's understanding of the latent content of the interaction with the object).

In this chapter I shall attempt to illustrate the importance of the way in which aspects of the interpretive process take the form of symbolic action on the part of the analyst and the ways in which these forms of interpretation are drawn from experiences in and of the analytic third. To this end, I shall offer three clinical vignettes each of which highlights a different aspect of interpretive action. In selecting this clinical material, I have made an effort to offer illustrations of the everyday and commonplace in analytic practice. Interpretive action is not an exceptional analytic event; it is simply part of the fabric of ordinary interpretive analytic work.

Clinical Illustration I: Silence as Interpretation of a Perversion of Language and Thought

Dr. M., an English-born research scientist in her early forties, entered analysis because she was experiencing overwhelming anxiety that she would lose her job and "end up disgraced and in the gutter." She feared that it would be discovered that for years she had been getting by at work by "piecing together" bits of advice and information gleaned from conversations with her colleagues. Her whole career felt like a sham that was in imminent danger of unraveling.

In the years preceding the beginning of analysis, the patient had been twice married (and twice divorced), both times to men from socially prominent families whom she had found to be extremely handsome. During sex, the patient felt no sexual arousal of her own, but took great pleasure in the power that she experienced in being able to arouse her husband to a great pitch of sexual excitement. Having succeeded in doing so, she would then consciously imagine that she was stealing his erect penis in the act of intercourse. In this fantasy, the patient silently observed the scene from a great psychological distance. Since the demonstration of the intensity of her husband's sexual excitement was so critical a part of the sexual scene for Dr. M., she would encourage her sexual partner to physical extremes that once led her second husband to accidentally fracture one of her ribs during intercourse.

In the initial year of the analysis, Dr. M. at the end of each session would tell me that she would see me the next day and name the specific time of our session. This was done with the conscious intention of reminding me that we had a session scheduled for the following day and what time that session was to begin. This "reminder" (an unspoken accusation that I would forget the session unless reminded) served as a powerful way of provoking anger in me. The patient held the conscious conviction that causing me to become angry was one of the few ways she had of eliciting interest in her or even memory of her.

As the analysis proceeded, it became increasingly apparent that Dr. M. did not speak for the sake of reflecting on her internal life or commenting on present or past experience. She seemed to have virtually no interest in anything that she might think, feel, or say. The act of talking seemed to serve only one function: to get *me* to talk. When I pointed this out to Dr. M., she, without hesitation, acknowledged that this was so. The patient felt that the only events in the analysis that held any importance for her were the interventions I made, whether they be confrontations, interpretations, or clarifications. Even my questions were felt to be of value because they reflected the way I thought and what I considered to be of importance. The patient kept a journal in which she recorded the events of every meeting. Years later, she told me that she wrote down only what she could remember of what I had said and did not have a single reference to any of her thoughts or comments. (I experienced Dr. M.'s ready confirmation of my interpretations as maddening since her unswerving, non-self-reflective matter-of-factness served as still another manifestation of the patient's exclusive interest in ferreting out my thoughts and comments.)

Over time, I made the interpretation that the patient felt that it was impossible for her to create anything of value and that this belief led her to behave as if the entire worth of the analysis lay in me. Moreover, the patient's fantasy of the process of analysis involved a vision of the patient's passively absorbing my internal strength through the ideas and feelings that I conveyed to her. She readily concurred that this was what she wanted and expected from analysis.

A history was presented in bits and pieces over several years. Dr. M. told me about childhood memories and fantasies in a way that suggested that the information was being given to me in order for me to help her with her difficulties while she remained utterly passive. In other words, these were not memories upon which she reflected or about which she experienced curiosity; rather, they were data handed over to me for the purpose of my making sense of them and interpreting them for her.

Dr. M. reported having had conscious childhood fantasies in which her idealized father (described at times as "wonderful" and at other times as depressed, withdrawn, and utterly dominated by his wife and his mother) was felt to be the sole source of the patient's value and strength. However, this strength was borrowed by the patient and could only be briefly held by her, never becoming her possession in any permanent, integrated way. As a child, Dr. M. developed a compulsively repeated form of play in which slips of paper, paper clips, bottle caps, and so on, were distributed in hiding places around the house and were used to represent "spells" that had been given to her by her father. Each spell would provide her a particular form of power, for example, the ability to run fast in a given fantasied race, act bravely in the face of a specific danger, demonstrate intelligence at a key moment, and so on. The temporary and uninte-grated nature of the "internalization" was reflected by the fact that the fragments of the father's power were named "spells," that is, magical, externally generated ego-dys-tonic forces.

Dr. M., the middle of three children, experienced her mother as hatefully withholding of her love for the patient while far more generously bestowing her affection on the patient's brother and sister. The patient was thought to be mentally retarded by her first-grade teacher, who suggested to Dr. M.'s parents that she undergo psychological testing. The tests revealed that the patient was of superior intelligence. Nonetheless, Dr. M. showed no signs of being able to read until she was in the third grade. (The patient had in fact learned to read in the second grade, but took pleasure in keeping this development a secret.)

For the sake of brevity, I shall describe what I came to understand in the course of the succeeding several years of work with Dr. M. without providing a detailed account of the analytic process within which this under-standing was developed. The patient seemed to experience my interpretations (and everything else I said) as "spells," as magical acts through which idealized (and at the same time, denigrated) internal contents were momentarily lent to her only to be immediately exhausted, leaving her as empty and impotent as before. Dr. M. attempted to conceal the joy and excitement with which she received an interpretation since she experienced the event as if she had succeeded in deceptively extracting, stealing, wooing, seducing, it from me. She feared that if I were to sense the quality of the satisfaction and excitement that she experienced, I would understand the desperate dependence she felt on me and would either be revolted and frightened by the enormity of her greed and excitement or would sadistically torment her and hold her hostage forever while stealing her money (her life) from her.

At the same time, Dr. M. resented the borrowed/stolen magical internal objects acquired from me. She felt me to be hateful in my tantalizing of her with these borrowed/stolen objects while I remained unwilling to release her from her dependence on me. She experienced me as cruelly withholding of my recognition of her as capable of having strengths (e.g., a sense of humor) other than those borrowed from me. Dr. M.'s angry attacks on the introjected parts of me (my interpretations) helped to establish a vicious cycle in which she remained unable to learn (unable to make use of anything I might say). (Each aspect of this form of relatedness and the underlying fantasies were fully and repeatedly interpreted and received by the patient in the way I have described.)

I came to view Dr. M.'s use of interpretation as a form of perversion in which she compulsively and excitedly transformed each of my interpretations into an eroticized magical spell. (It was only much later in the

analysis that the patient became fully aware that the
nature of the excitement she felt in receiving an interpretation was "like an electric charge through her that made
[her] body tingle." She eventually recognized this feeling
to be a form of sexual excitement.)

I understood the patient's use of my interventions as
an unconscious attempt to create a sense of a living self
from the borrowed/stolen contents of her parents. Even
interpretations concerning the patient's use of interpretation (i.e., the interpretation of the transference "in terms
of *total situations*" [Joseph 1985, Klein 1952b; see also
Chapter 8]) were immediately incorporated into the
perverse drama. In other words, each attempt to interpret
the patient's use of my talk for the purpose of bringing
herself to life in the way described was in turn transformed by the patient into still another scene in the
drama.

It took me quite some time to fully appreciate the
extent to which the form of relatedness just descibed
prevented Dr. M. from generating a single original
thought in the analytic discourse. I had underestimated
the extent of the patient's paralysis of thought. My
blindness to this aspect of the therapeutic interaction
resulted in part from the fact that Dr. M. was able to
describe her experience in a way that often gave the
appearance of insight and self-reflection. She was extremely attentive to certain kinds of detail about the
analytic setting, for example, noticing if the cushion on
the armchair in my office was rumpled in a way that
suggested that someone had been reclining in it in a
manner that she had not seen before: "There must have
been a new female patient 'lounging' seductively in your
chair." Such fantasies at first seemed rich, but over time
it became clear that the patient's fantasies were restricted

to a single theme with slight variations on it: a continual party was felt to be going on in my interpersonal life (e.g., my amorous relationship with my wife, my romantic and intellectual enjoyment of my patients, my flirtations and affairs with supervisees, etc.) and in my internal life (the interesting and insightful thoughts that I was thinking and the richness of my creativity).

In the course of the first five years of analysis, Dr. M. made substantial progress in several aspects of her life. For instance, she developed the capacity to learn in an academic setting, thus allowing her for the first time in her life to engage in research activity that reflected her own ideas. She made great strides in becoming a successful, creative, and respected member of her field. Her capacity to make decisions and manage her life had improved dramatically. However, her capacity to develop relationships with both men and women remained stunted. The satisfaction she derived from the interpersonal aspects of her work made her aware in a new way of how unable she was to develop either romantic/sexual relationships with men or close friendships with women. (Despite the fact that Dr. M. had developed the capacity to experience sexual excitement that she felt to be her own and was able to exprience orgasm for the first time in her life, she was not able to have an intimate and exciting relationship with men whom she liked and respected.)

Dr. M. had become aware of her loneliness in a way that she described as "agonizing." She could now more fully experience and observe aspects of the central conflict constituting the transference–countertransference: she felt unbearably lonely and desperately wanted to "let me in," but at the same time felt so enraged at me for my "unwillingness to help [her]" (i.e., to think for her) that she vowed that she would never allow herself to submit to me by treating me as a "real person." She at times commented that she felt so furious at me that she was genuinely surprised that none of my patients had yet murdered me.

Despite the psychological changes that had occurred in some sectors of the patient's life, the perversion of the interpretive process continued in the analysis and resulted in the foreclosure of a generative discourse of a sustained sort. When such discourse would briefly take place, it was invariably followed by weeks or months of withdrawal on the part of the patient into an intensified attack on the analytic discourse through an enactment of a now con-sciously fantasied "arid" discourse/intercourse involving a tantalizing and ultimately powerless father and an un-touchable mother. This lifeless discourse/intercourse was observed from afar by the patient in her role as excluded and excited child pretending not to understand what she was seeing (her "pseudo mental retardation").

In a session during this phase of work, I offered an interpretation concerning the sequence of engagement and anxious withdrawal that I have just described. The patient responded by asking me a series of questions about my interpretation: Did I feel that this was some-thing that she did every time she began to be present in the room with me? How could she prevent herself from withdrawing in the way that I described? Did I think she had done this from the beginning of the analysis or was I referring only to the current meeting or perhaps to the last few meetings? An emotional shift occurred in me at this point that led me to respond differently from the way I had previously. Instead of experiencing anger, I felt sadness and a deep sense of despair. This transference-countertransference shift contributed to my decision to embark on a course of interpretation largely conveyed in the form of action.

I met each of the patient's questions in the session being described with a form of silence that both the patient and I experienced as having an unmistakably different quality from other instances of silence that had occurred previously in the analysis. The silences in the current hour were filled with an intensity of feeling that served as an interpretation that could not have been made in words because of the perversion of language that was being enacted in the analysis. This new form of silence constituted an interpretive action, an interpretation that was not comprised of words and therefore lay (to some degree) outside the domain of the power of the perverse transformation of language. In the transference-counter-transference, the perversion involved my playing the role of the idealized/impotent father while the patient was predominantly identified with the impenetrable mother and the hidden, observing, envious, excluded, overexcited child.

The silences under discussion were intended to convey an understanding that had been developed and presented to the patient many times in the course of the analysis, but had to this juncture been immediately and systematically transformed and rendered ineffectual as the patient incorporated them into the next scene of the perverse drama. The meanings conveyed by my deliberate silence (which meanings I articulated for myself) included the idea that the patient knew full well that her questions were not offered as a part of a discourse in which she was attempting to develop greater understanding of herself for purposes of psychological growth; rather, her questions represented an angry accusation that I was hatefully excluding her from the riches of my internal world (in the maternal and paternal transference) that she both wished to plunder and hoard and at the same time enviously attack and spoil. She also knew that if I were to answer her questions, she would feel momentary relief in possessing one of these parts of me (one of my spells), but would almost immediately come to feel infuriated with me. Her anger would reflect her feeling that I was forcing on her an enslavement to me by preventing her from developing the capacity to create thoughts, feelings, and sensations that she could experience as her own.

Dr. M.'s initial response to my silence/interpretation was to fire more and more angry/provocative questions at me. She then shifted to a series of affectless descriptions of current events in her life as if attempting to comply with what she felt to be a demand on her to conduct the analysis by herself without any help from me. (The sadness and despair in me continued and was increasingly accompanied by a deep sense of loneliness. I could feel the futility of the patient's frenzied thrashing about. For the first time, I was not at all convinced I could be of help to her.)

Dr. M. began the next hour by announcing that she was having great financial difficulties and would have to diminish the frequency of our sessions from five to four meetings per week. This represented a rather transparent provocation in an effort to extract words (spells) from me. I felt that any effort that I might make at interpreting the patient's anger and feelings of isolation in conjunction with her efforts at extracting spells from me would simply perpetuate the perverse drama. Consequently, I chose to interpret with silence, despite the danger that I might be exchanging one form of perverse drama for another, that is, reversing the roles in a sadomasochistic relationship and further intensifying the patient's (and my own) feelings of isolation. I also for the first time considered the possibility of the patient's committing suicide. Again, the silence was meant to convey my sense that the patient could make an interpretation of the transference for herself and that her not doing so reflected a form of perversion of language and thought that was currently being enacted between us. The measure of the value of the silence as interpretive action would lie in the degree to which the silence served to expand analytic space. In other words, would the silence facilitate the capacity for symbolization of conscious and unconscious experience (enrich the "dialectic of modes of generating experience" [Ogden 1989a]) or would the silence foreclose the use of symbols and reduce the analytic interaction to a series of reflexive evacuations of unmediated experiences of isolation (that the patient was not yet capable of experiencing as sadness)? Intermittently during this period, I told the patient that I thought we both knew that my thinking for her would create the illusion of an analysis, but that nothing would come of an endless repetition of my substituting my own thoughts for what might become her own capacity to think and to feel her own thoughts, feelings, and sensations. This was an idea that I had discussed with Dr. M. many times over the previous years. Nonetheless, I felt that it was important that I continue to present to her my understanding of my reasons for conducting myself in the analysis in the way that I was (Boyer 1983, personal communication).

A session several months later was unique in that silence as interpretive action became the principal context for, as well as the content of, the session. Dr. M. experienced in a much fuller and clearer way than she

had at any previous time in the analysis the elements of
the internal conflict that to this point had been given
shape almost exclusively in the form of the perversion of
language and thought that has been described. Dr. M.
talked about events in her current work life that were
undergoing change for the better as a result of her ability
to experience herself as a person who had the right to
speak and behave as an authority (someone who could
think and speak her thoughts). She interrupted herself by
saying, "Okay, I've wanted a response from you at every
moment today. I *am* curious about why I need to hear
your response to every single one of the sentences that I
utter." (I had asked Dr. M. in a previous session whether
she had felt curious about her behavior in a situation that
she was describing.) After three minutes of silence, the
patient again protested that she could not think—she
could sleep, but she could not think. I was interested by
her reference to sleep and (silently) wondered if she had
begun to be able to remember her dreams. The patient
had reported very few dreams to this point in the analysis
and those that had been reported were presented with
either no associations at all or with mechanical imitations
of associations.

Dr. M. went through her usual maneuvers in an
effort to get me to talk, but there was something subtly
different about her that I could not name. In the middle
of the session, Dr. M. looked around the office (but did
not turn on the couch to look at me) and asked, "Have
you changed your office?" I made no reply. "It looks like
it's been moving laterally. The cracks on the wall have
gotten bigger. What do you think?"

Despite the fact that half of the patient's sentences
were questions, she did not seem to expect/demand
responses from me. More importantly, there was some-

thing quite imaginative and humorously self-mocking in
what she was saying and in the way she was saying it. Her
sense of the change in the relationship with me was being
described in the physical-sensory experience of a change
in the analytic space—there was movement occurring in
the present moment that had the quality of a "lateral"
movement (a pun on "literal" movement) in the analytic
space and a decrease in the density of the barriers to
reflective discourse (the widening cracks in the wall). To
have offered my understanding of the meaning of these
comments would have usurped the beginning of Dr. M.'s
capacity for imaginative thought and most likely would
have caused the patient to return to the familiar ground
of the repetition in the transference of a perverse dependence on me as the source of all that is good and valuable.

The patient began the following day's session by
saying that she had had a dream the previous night.
When she awoke from it in the middle of the night she
considered writing it down, but felt that it was so vivid
that she could not possibly forget it. She said that she was
now unable to remember anything of the dream.

I said that it seemed that she had begun to think in
her sleep, but was anxious about the prospect of thinking
while with me. She said she was certain that the dream
was about her being unable to think, but did not know
why she felt convinced of this. Dr. M. went on to say that
she was losing weight and was approaching a weight
where she "loses her breasts." (I felt she was accusing me
of willfully shrinking my own breasts so that there would
be no milk for her. I imagined that she felt that both of us
would rather starve to death [kill the analysis] than give
anything [or lose anything] to the other.) Dr. M. added
that she was certain that I had not noticed her weight loss.
The session was filled with angry attempts to get me to

give her interpretations. She at one point demanded that I tell her how much time we had left in the hour despite the fact that she was wearing a watch. I said that reading the time on her own watch would not be the same as my telling her the time. She barked back, "No, that wouldn't help me. I want to know *your* time. My time isn't of any help to me. Your time is the only time that counts." (Dr. M. had previously told me that she never knows the correct time because she kept every clock and watch that she owned at slightly different times.)

The session continued with more questions from the patient that were "interpreted" to the patient with silence and to myself in words. (An important aspect of interpretive action is the analyst's consistent formulation for himself of the evolving interpretation in verbal terms. In the absence of such efforts, the idea of interpretive action can degenerate into the analyst's rationalization for impulsive, non-self-reflective acting out.)

Near the end of the session, the patient recounted having seen a homeless person the previous evening begging for money as she and her parents were about to enter a very elegant restaurant. (In my own mind I understood the scene as a description of the patient's feeling of intense deprivation in the session with me.) The patient then said she could now remember the dream that she had had the previous night. In it, a man was pouring expensive champagne into her glass in the restaurant at which they had dined. The champagne was glamorous and sparkling, but went flat a moment after it entered the glass. The patient awoke from the dream in a state of intense anxiety.

Dr. M. said, "That's how I feel with you, I feel desperate, like a homeless person and would kill you if I had the guts, but when you give me something, it feels

flat almost immediately after you give it to me. I must kill
it in some way, but I don't know how I do it or why."
(Although there was remarkable vitality in the initial
parts of Dr. M.'s statement, the latter part of the patient's
comments regarding her own role in attacking my interpretations seemed rote and compliant to me.)

Dr. M. did not immediately follow her comment
with a question as she had consistently done in the past.
However, after a short pause, she returned to asking
me for the time in a way that invited me to interpret the
connection between this demand, the imagery of the
dream, and the account of the homeless person. I again
responded with silence that was intended to renew the
interpretive working through of the perversion of language and thought.

The analytic movement (experienced by the patient
in the form of the experience of physical movement of my
office) continued in this phase of the work. Striking
among the changes in the analytic process that occurred
was the appearance for the first time in the analysis of
several slips of the tongue in almost every session. The
patient was not only embarrassed by the slips, but also
seemed to welcome them and experience interest in them.
For instance, in talking about the incomparable pleasure
she derived from the feeling of power that she felt when
she succeeded in extracting an interpretation from me,
Dr. M. unconsciously substituted the word "powder" for
"power." She associated "powder" to the ashes resulting
from a cremation and to her feelings of deadness and
extreme detachment that were inseparable (and at times
indistinguishable) from the sexual excitement connected
with acquiring one of my spells. Most importantly, there
was a distinct sense generated in this exchange that these
were thoughts that were the patient's thoughts, although I

made no comment about this in an effort not to change her thoughts into something other than what she had created. It seemed that "despite herself," in these slips Dr. M. was unconsciously allowing herself to begin to experience and create a voice for aspects of herself that had been present to this point in the analysis only in a strangulated, stillborn form, that is, in the form of the transference-countertransference relationship organized around the perversion of language and thought that has been discussed.

Clinical Illustration II: Interpretive Action as an Early Stage of Interpretation

During the telephone call prior to our first session, Mr. P. told me that his marriage of 18 years was in shambles, that he was in love with and having an "intensely passionate" affair with the wife of his best friend, and that his life was "in a downhill spiral." As the patient entered my consulting room for the initial session, he had the look of a broken man. The intensity of his desperateness and anxiety filled the room. Mr. P. handed me a sheaf of papers and explained that these were love poems that he had collected that he thought would help me to understand the feelings that he was having in relation to the woman he had mentioned to me on the phone. The abject surrender that was conveyed in the patient's facial expression and bodily movements as he handed me the papers had the effect of a plea; it felt as if it would be cruel and inhumane not to accept his gesture. I was aware that there was something slightly effeminate about the patient's appearance and manner of speech.

Immediately following these momentary initial impressions, but still within the period of seconds during which the patient's hand was outstretched, I developed a distinct sense that the patient was inviting me to engage in a type of sadomasochistic homosexual scene. In this scene, I imagined that I would either submit to him and have his "loving" contents (concretely represented by the poems) forced into me or I would be moved to sadistically refuse these contents and thereby demonstrate my power over him (perhaps through a "forceful" interpretation of the patient's wish to dump his destructive internal objects into me).

On the basis of these extremely rapid (hardly verbally symbolized) responses to what was unfolding in the opening seconds of the analysis, I said to Mr. P. that it would take some time to understand something of what had just transpired between us and so I suggested that he keep the poems for now. In the minutes that followed, I became increasingly aware that I had not wanted to touch the papers that Mr. P. had offered to me and had felt an even stronger aversion to the idea of touching Mr. P.'s hand. I had felt that to have accepted the papers would have been to have taken part in the particular form of sexual fantasy that I sensed underlay what was being enacted in his occupying the bed of his best friend. I hypothesized in a highly condensed, hardly articulated way that in having an affair with his best friend's wife, Mr. P. had in unconscious fantasy put his penis where his best friend's/father's penis had been. In this way, he had had sex with his father while avoiding conscious awareness of the homosexuality of the act because the meeting of his father's penis and his own took place in his mother's vagina.

I view my thoughts/hypotheses about the inces-
tuous/homosexual meaning of what had just occurred in
the session as a form of "reverie" (Bion 1962a) that
reflected experience in (of) an intersubjective analytic
third that was being generated by Mr. P. and myself in
the course of Mr. P.'s introduction of himself to me. I am
mentioning these thoughts for two reasons. First, they
formed the basis for more fully elaborated transference
interpretations that were discussed with the patient in
small bits later in the hour and in the succeeding several
sessions regarding the patient's anxiety about beginning
analysis with me. The conscious level of the patient's
anxieties (that were discussed by Mr. P. later in the hour)
related to his fears of breaches of confidentiality, the
fantasy of meeting me in situations outside of the analytic
setting, and his already knowing things about me from
my writing that excited him and made him feel we could
have a special relationship with one another.

Second, I mention these reveries/hypotheses because I feel that these thoughts and feelings would not
have been discernible to me had I reflexively acceded to
the patient's offer of the poems in an "empathic" effort to
accept his expression of his need to be understood. Not
accepting the poems allowed a psychological space to be
created in which the poems could be created (and eventually understood) as an "analytic object" (Green 1975;
see also Chapter 5). The intervention (the act of not
accepting the poems, in conjunction with the tone and
content of my comments to Mr. P. about my reasons for
not accepting them) represented not simply a way to
attempt to create "analytic space" (Ogden 1986, Viderman 1979); in addition, it represented an early stage of
interpretation that communicated the essential elements

of what would in the course of several meetings be offered as a set of verbally symbolized interpretations. The interpretation in action represented a form of communication of my initial, tentative understanding of the following unconscious transference-countertransference meanings: the intensity and desperateness of the patient's need to put something into me (the papers into my hand, the poetry into my mind and body) reflected his feeling that he could not bear to live with the destructive, out of control passion and fear that he felt to be consuming him. He felt that it was imperative that the destructive passion be evacuated into me so that he could be freed of it while remaining connected with it in me. At the same time, I felt that Mr. P. wished to make use of me as an analyst in his effort to extricate himself from the web of painful internal and external object relationships in which he felt hopelessly trapped. All of this was discussed with the patient in pieces in the course of the first few sessions, using language very similar to that which I have used here.

To summarize, my rather prosaic statement that it would take some time to understand something of what had transpired between Mr. P. and me, and my suggestion that he keep his poems for the time being, represented more than an effort to establish an analytic space within which to think about what was being enacted. As importantly, the statement represented a form of transference interpretation in the form of action that emerged from my experience in (and of) the intersubjective analytic third.

My experience in and of the intersubjective third had led me to formulate the opening interaction of the analysis in terms of unconscious incestuous/homosexual fantasies by which the patient felt in danger of being overwhelmed. His attempt to hand me the love poems was a highly specific communication about his internal object world.

The semantic content of the words I used did not delineate my hypothesis concerning the incestuous/homosexual nature of the unconscious fantasy in which I was being invited to participate. To have offered the interpretation to the patient in a verbally symbolized form at that point would have been to participate in the fantasied sexual drama in the role of the invasive homosexual partner. Nonetheless, my refusal to accept the poems was more than a generic refusal to engage in an acting-in with a patient; it was a refusal to take part in the particular unconscious fantasy being experienced in the analytic third (which experience I was formulating for myself in a verbally symbolic form). As a result, my verbal action carried meanings (tentative understandings of the transference-countertransference) that constituted an early stage of what would later be offered to the patient as a verbally symbolized transference interpretation. (The subsequent elaboration in words of the understanding initially offered in the form of an interpretive action, as well as the exploration of the meaning to the analysand of the experience of the interpretive action itself, are inextricable parts of this form of interpretive intervention.)

Clinical Illustration III: Interpretive Action in the Area of Transitional Phenomena

In the following example, interpretation in action was offered in the context of a transference-countertransference field in which transitional phenomena (Winnicott 1951) were of central importance. Although the interpretation that will be discussed was presented in the form of a question, the meaning of the interpretation was carried as much by *the experience of the intervention as a transitional phenomenon* as it was by the semantic content of the words.

Dr. L., an analyst in consultation with me, had presented over a period of years a rather difficult case from her practice. The patient, Ms. D., an extremely intelligent woman in her early thirties, had been so crippled by phobias (particularly claustrophobia) and anxiety about her inability to think that she had never been able to work nor had she been able to pursue graduate-level education. (It had taken her eight years to complete an undergraduate degree.) In addition to the phobic symptoms, the patient engaged in compulsive masturbation in which the central fantasy involved being sexually stimulated by several men against her will (usually while she was bound or being threatened). Although the patient occasionally entered into relationships with men, she had had no sexual experiences other than masturbation.

Ms. D. arrived at a session in her fourth year of analysis saying that a friend had given her one of the analyst's published articles on psychoanalysis. The patient's friend, who was a graduate student in psychology, had not known the name of Ms. D.'s analyst, since the identity of the analyst was for the patient a closely guarded (shameful) secret. Ms. D. said that she had not yet read the article because she wanted to discuss her feelings about it, and hear the analyst's thoughts with regard to her reading it, before going ahead.

The patient said that she would like to read the paper although she was afraid that she would not understand it. The analyst was aware of feeling anxious about the patient's viewing a discourse (between herself and her colleagues) that felt private. Dr. L. told me that she had had the fantasy that she would never again be able to write once this private area had been invaded by the patient. The analyst also had fantasies that the patient would recognize herself in the article despite the fact that Dr. L. had never written about her work with Ms. D.

In the consultation in which Dr. L. discussed this session with me, these countertransference feelings were understood as a reflection of an unconscious fantasy (on the part of Dr. L.) that the patient had discovered Dr. L.'s shameful secret of wishing to observe in an excited state her own parents' intercourse. The result would be not only the punishment of being paralyzed in her writing (the recording of her "insights"), but also of being "found out" by the patient.

The patient's feelings of shame about being in analysis had been tentatively understood and interpreted over time as having roots in the patient's unconsciously fantasied equation of the analytic space and the parental bedroom into which the patient felt she was secretly and excitedly entering. Although the patient discussed the elements of this understanding with considerable interest, it seemed to Dr. L. that Ms. D. was "viewing the interpretations from the outside." In a session some weeks after the patient had been given the journal article, Ms. D. said that she had read the paper and had found it interesting to hear the analyst's voice in this different form. Ms. D.'s excitement as well as her feelings of competitiveness, envy, and guilt were discussed in some detail. The patient then said that there were several terms and ideas that she had not understood and would like to know more about them. The analyst asked the patient, "What would you like to know?" Dr. L. became aware of

the ambiguity of her question only after she had posed it.
Did she intend to answer any and all of the patient's
questions, or was she simply inquiring about the nature
of the questions the patient had? Dr. L. told me that in
the moment of asking this question she had created in her
own mind the imaginative possibility of directly answering the patient's questions, although she had felt no
pressure to make a decision about whether or not she
would actually do so.

Ms. D. was startled by the analyst's question (responding to the same ambiguity of which the analyst had
become aware) and said that she did not know if the
analyst really meant what she had said. (Ms. D. had
during the course of the analysis repeatedly described the
loneliness that she had felt during her childhood in not
being able to talk to either of her parents or to her siblings
about "What the hell is going on?" "What did you mean
by that?" "Why did he [her father] say that?" etc.) Ms. D.
went on to say that she felt that something important had
changed between Dr. L. and herself as a result of Dr. L.'s
response (which she had not at all expected). The patient
said that she no longer knew what to ask or even if she
wanted to ask anything. Ms. D. paused and said that
mostly what she had wanted to know was whether the
analyst would be willing to talk to her about the things
she was confused about, and surprisingly, the answers to
the questions no longer seemed to matter.

Dr. L. understood the patient's response in terms of
Ms. D.'s conflicted wish to be curious about the private
discourse (including the sexual intercourse) of her parents
without feeling consumed by it or entrapped in it. The
patient was struggling to create in the transference-
countertransference an intersubjective "potential space"
(Winnicott 1971b; see also Ogden 1985) in which imagined participation in the parental discourse/intercourse

could take place in a different way. In other words, Ms.
D. was attempting to be curious (to imagine and think
about the parental discourse/intercourse) without becoming caught in a perverse, overstimulating psychological event that would have to be either compulsively and
excitedly repeated (as in the compulsive masturbation) or
fearfully warded off (e.g., by a paralysis of the capacity
for thought).

Dr. L.'s response, "What would you like to know?"
was spontaneous and highly informed by her experience
in the intersubjective analytic third. This intervention
stands in contrast to an inquiry into or interpretation of
the nature of the patient's conflicted unconscious wish to
participate in the extra-analytic (sexual) life of the analyst. Dr. L.'s response represented an interpretation in
action that was generated in a potential space between
reality and fantasy. Dr. L.'s response (interpretive action)
conveyed understandings that were utilizable by the
patient in a way that had not previously been possible
because the response itself represented a form of transitional phenomenon, that is, an intersubjectively created
experience in which an emotionally important paradox
was created and maintained without having to be resolved. In this instance the paradox related to the *latent*
question (within Dr. L.'s manifest question): "Do you
'really' want to participate in the private intercourse/dis-
course of your parents/analyst?" The question in both its
manifest and latent content was re-created intersubjectively in such a way that both analyst and analysand came
to experience and understand it as a question (more
accurately, a set of questions) for which no answer was
required.

Under other circumstances, Dr. L.'s response/inter-
pretive action might have been heard as a frightening,
overstimulating invitation to "break the law of the father"

(Lacan 1957), that is, to violate the prohibition against breaches of personal boundaries that are at the foundation of the analytic relationship. The fact that Ms. D. experienced the analyst's interpretive action/question as having the qualities of a transitional phenomenon (an intersubjectively created paradox in the form of a question that need not be answered) was reflected in Ms. D.'s response to the intervention: she did not attempt to compulsively enact voyeuristic fantasies or to actually attempt to further enter into the professional discourse of the analyst (for example, by anxiously seeking out other writings of Dr. L.).

In this instance, the analyst's formulation of the interpretation in words for herself evolved over time. There was a spontaneous, unplanned quality to the intervention/question, the meanings of which the analyst only began to be able to recognize and consciously formulate for herself in words after (or perhaps as) the question was being posed. This type of interpretive action might be thought of as representing "the spontaneous gesture of the analytic third." Dr. L.'s understanding of her question as a type of transitional phenomenon that generated paradoxical, imaginative possibilities became fully articulated for herself only in the course of consultation.

To conclude, the interpretive action under discussion conveyed an understanding of the patient's unconscious conflict (as experienced in and through the intersubjective analytic third) and represented an experience in the area of transitional phenomena. In this instance, it was necessary for *the experience of the interpretive action itself* to occupy a transitional space wherein new imaginative (as opposed to compulsively fantasied) possibilities could be created intersubjectively. The question, "What would you like to know?" represented an interpretive action that conveyed an understanding of the patient's leading unconscious conflict in such a way that a psychological shift resulted in which the primal scene (and the oedipal drama) could be safely (re-)created and explored in an area between reality and fantasy. In that "third area of experiencing" (Winnicott 1951), neither Dr. L.'s nor the patient's (manifest and latent) questions needed to be answered. In fact, it was the conveying of this understanding (i.e., that the questions required no answer) that constituted the interpretation.

Summary

In this chapter the concept of interpretive action is understood as the analyst's use of activity to convey specific aspects of his understanding of the transference-countertransference that cannot be communicated to the patient in the form of verbally symbolic speech alone at the juncture in the analysis when the interpretation-in-action is made. The understanding of the transference-countertransference conveyed by an interpretive action is derived from the experience of analyst and analysand in the intersubjective analytic third. Although the analyst uses action to communicate aspects of his understanding of the transference-countertransference to the analysand, the analyst simultaneously formulates the interpretation in words for himself.

The three clinical illustrations of interpretive action that have been presented were selected not because they represent remarkable or unusual psychoanalytic events. Rather, they have been presented in an effort to illustrate the way in which interpretation-in-action represents a fundamental, and yet insufficiently explored, aspect of the psychoanalytic interpretive process.

8

Analyzing the Matrix of the Transference–Countertransference

The analyst must have a theoretical framework with which to conceptualize not only the nature of the relationships between transference figures occupying the analytic stage, but also the matrix (or background experiential state) within which the transference–countertransference is being generated.

Over the past forty years there has been an expanding appreciation of the importance of the analytic context, not simply as a framework for the containment of the analytic process, but as a pivotal dimension of the transference–countertransference. Melanie Klein (1952b), for example, stressed that one must "think in terms of *total situations* transferred from the past to the present as well as emotional defences and object relations" (p. 55). Betty Joseph (1985) has elaborated on this idea: "By definition transference must include everything that the patient brings to the relationship. What he brings in can best be gauged by our focusing our attention on what is going on within the relationship, how he is using the analyst, alongside and beyond what he is saying" (p. 447).

Winnicott's (1949, 1958a, 1963) conception of the "environment-mother" has greatly enhanced the analytic conception of "the matrix of transference" (1958a, p. 33). The infant not only has a relationship with the mother as object, but also from the beginning has a relationship with the mother as environment. Consequently, transference is not simply a transferring of one's experience of one's internal objects onto external objects; it is as importantly a transferring of one's experience of the internal environment within which one lives onto the analytic situation. (Among those who have contributed to the development of the concept of transference to the mother-as-environment are Balint [1968], Bion [1962a], Bollas [1987], Boyer [1983], R. Gaddini [1987], Giovacchini [1979], Green [1975], Grotstein [1981], Kernberg [1985], Langs [1978], Loewald [1960], McDougall [1974], Modell [1976], Pontalis [1972], Reider [1953], Searles [1960], Viderman [1974], and Volkan [1976].)

In this chapter, I shall discuss an aspect of the analytic context that is related to, but distinct from, those elements addressed by Klein, Winnicott, and those who have extended and elaborated on their work. I shall take as my focus an exploration of the way in which experience in general, and transference–countertransference experience in particular, is the outcome of the interplay of three modes of creating psychological meaning: the autistic-contiguous, the paranoid-schizoid, and the depressive. The dynamic interplay of these modes of generating experience determines the nature of the background state of being (or psychological matrix) within which one is living and constructing personal meanings at any given moment. As a result, an understanding of these modes of generating experience and the experiential states associated with them is essential to an understanding and interpretation of the transference–countertransference.

I shall begin by briefly summarizing my own understanding of the three fundamental background states of being constituting the context of all human experience including the transference–countertransference. I shall then present several fragments of analytic work that illustrate some of the ways in which psychoanalytic technique is shaped by the analyst's understanding of the predominant (but ever-shifting) mode or modes of experience forming the context of the transference-countertransference.

Dimensions of Experience

All human experience, including transference–countertransference experience, can be thought of as the outcome of the dialectical interplay of three modes of creating and organizing psychological meaning. Each of these modes is associated with one of three fundamental psychological organizations — the depressive position, the paranoid-schizoid position, and the autistic-contiguous position.[1] (The depressive and the paranoid-schizoid positions are concepts introduced by Melanie Klein [1935, 1946, 1952c, 1957, 1958] while the autistic-contiguous position is a conception that I have introduced in previous communications [Ogden 1988, 1989a,b] as an elaboration and extension of the work of Bick [1968, 1986], Meltzer [1975, 1986; Meltzer et al. 1975] and Tustin [1972, 1980, 1981, 1984, 1986].) None of the three modes exists in isolation from the others: each creates, preserves, and negates the others dialectically. Each mode generates an experiential state characterized by its own distinctive form of anxiety, types of

___

1. It is beyond the scope of the present discussion to offer more than a schematic overview of the major psychological organizations and the dialectical interplay between them. For a more detailed discussion of these topics see Ogden (1985, 1986, 1988, 1989a,b).

defense, degree of subjectivity, form of object relatedness, type of internalization process, and so on.

The *autistic-contiguous* position is associated with the most primitive mode of attributing meaning to experience. It is a psychological organization in which the experience of self is based upon the ordering of sensory experience, particularly sensation at the skin surface (cf. Bick 1968, 1986). In an autistic-contiguous mode, the predominant anxiety is that of the collapse of the sense of sensory-boundedness upon which the rudiments of the experience of a cohesive self are based. This loss of boundedness is experienced as the terror of falling or leaking into endless, shapeless space (D. Rosenfeld 1984). The individual often attempts to defend himself against this type of anxiety by means of "second skin formation" (Bick 1968, 1986). Examples of defensive efforts of this sort include tenacious eye contact, continuous and unrelenting talk, compulsive wrapping of oneself in many layers of clothing, and so on.

The experience of objects in an autistic-contiguous realm is primarily in the form of "relationships" to autistic shapes (Tustin 1984) and autistic objects (Tustin 1980). These autistic phenomena are quite different from the shapes and objects that we ordinarily think of as constituting the object world. An autistic shape is a "felt-shape" (Tustin 1984) consisting of the idiosyncratic sensory impressions that an object makes as it touches the surface of our skin. For example, a rubber ball is not the round object we perceive in a visual and tactile way; rather, it is the feeling of an area (the beginnings of a place) of firm softness that is created as the object is held against the skin. Autistic shapes are predominantly experiences of soft objects (devoid of any sense of "thingness") and bodily substances (for example, saliva, feces, and urine). Such primitive "object-related" experiences (experiences of contiguity of surfaces) are soothing and calming in nature.

In contrast, "relationships" to autistic objects are experiences of hardness and edgedness that create the sensory experience of a protective crust or armor. For example, the experience of an autistic object may be created by pressing a hard, metallic object such as a key into the palm of one's hand. One does not feel the pain of a key digging into one's skin; rather, one feels the safety of having (being) a shell.

In the autistic-contiguous position, psychological change is mediated in large part by the process of imitation (as opposed to incorporation, introjection, and identification, which all require a more fully developed sense of an inner space into which qualities of the other can, in fantasy, be taken [cf. E. Gaddini 1969]). In imitation, the qualities of the external object are felt to alter one's surface, thus allowing one to be "shaped by" or "to carry" attributes of the object.

The *paranoid-schizoid* position (Klein 1946, 1952c, 1957, 1958; see also Ogden 1979, 1982a, 1986) generates a more mature, differentiated state of being than that associated with the autistic-contiguous position. The paranoid-schizoid dimension of experience is characterized by a form of subjectivity in which the self is experienced predominantly as "the self as object." In this experiential state there is very little sense of oneself as the author of one's thoughts and feelings. Instead, thoughts and feelings are experienced as forces and physical objects that occupy and bombard oneself. While the autistic-contiguous position can be thought of as presymbolic, the paranoid-schizoid position is characterized by a form of symbolization (termed *symbolic equation* [Segal 1957]) in which there is little capacity to differentiate between symbol and symbolized. In other words, there is almost no interpreting "I" interposed between oneself and one's lived experience. As a result there is an intense sense of immediacy to one's experience. In the absence of a sense that experience can be thought about, psychological defense tends to be enactive and evacuative in nature. One attempts to separate the endangering and endangered aspects of self and object (splitting) and to make use of others to experience that which one finds too dangerous to experience for oneself (projective identification).

In a paranoid-schizoid mode, the individual has achieved only a rudimentary sense of himself as an interpreting subject and therefore, the other is similarly experienced as an object as opposed to a subject. Consequently, there is little capacity for concern for the other; one can value objects, but one cannot have concern for even one's most valued possessions. In the absence of the capacity for concern, guilt remains outside of the emotional vocabulary of this experiential state. Lost objects are not mourned for, they are (in phantasy) magically repaired or re-created.

This is a relatively ahistorical experiential state since the use of splitting renders one's experience of oneself (in relation to one's objects) discontinuous. A beloved object who is suddenly absent is not experienced as a frighteningly unpredictable good object, but as a bad object. In this way, one's loving self and objects are kept safely disconnected from one's hated and hating self and objects. The result is a continual rewriting of history and a rapidly shifting sense of self and object. With each new affective experience of the object, one "unmasks" the other and discovers the "truth" about who the object is and always has been. Anxiety in this realm of experience takes the form of the fear of impending annihilation and fragmentation resulting from the destruction of loving aspects of self and object by hated and hating aspects of self and object.

The *depressive position* (Klein 1935, 1958; see also Ogden 1986) is the most mature, symbolically mediated psychological organization. In a depressive mode, there is a much more fully developed sense of an interpreting self standing between oneself and one's lived experience. In this experiential state, one's thoughts, feelings, and perceptions do not simply happen like "a clap of thunder or a hit" (Winnicott 1960b, p. 141); one's thoughts and feelings are experienced as one's own psychic creations that can be thought about and lived with and need not be immediately discharged in action or evacuated in omnipotent fantasy.

As the individual is increasingly able to experience himself as a subject, he also begins to recognize (by means of projection and identification) that his objects are also subjects who have an inner world of thoughts, feelings, and perceptions similar to one's own. As a result of one's growing awareness of the subjectivity of the other, it becomes possible to experience concern for the other; one knows that the other feels pain that is as real as one's own and that that pain cannot be magically undone or repaired. With the development of the capacity for concern comes the capacity for guilt, remorse, and the wish to make nonmagical reparation for the actual and phantasied harm that one has done.

As reliance on omnipotent defenses is relinquished in the depressive position, historicity is created. As has been discussed, in a paranoid-schizoid mode, history is continually being defensively rewritten. In the depressive position, for better or for worse, one is stuck in the present. Past experiences can be remembered and at times reinterpreted, but the past remains immutable. There is sadness, for example, in the knowledge that one's childhood will never be as one wishes it had been, but one's rootedness in time lends stability to one's sense of self.

In summary, the three positions that have been discussed represent dimensions of all human experience. No single realm of experience is ever encountered in pure form, any more than one ever encounters consciousness disconnected from unconsciousness. Each dimension of experience is created and negated by the others. The autistic-contiguous mode provides

much of the "sensory floor" (Grotstein 1987) of experience; the
paranoid-schizoid mode generates a good deal of the immediacy and vitality of concretely symbolized experience; the
depressive mode allows for the creation of an historical,
interpreting self. The three positions are related to one another
both diachronically and synchronically. That is, there is a
chronological, sequential relationship between the three positions (a developmental progression from the primitive to the
mature, from the presymbolic to the symbolic, from the pre-
subjective to the subjective, from the ahistorical to the historical, etc.). At the same time, the three positions have a
relationship of interactive simultaneity in that all three modes
of experience represent dimensions of every human experience.

   With this theoretical background, I will now clinically
illustrate some of the ways in which an understanding of the
three modes of generating experience informs the manner in
which we as analysts listen to, understand, and attempt to talk
with our patients. In particular, I shall focus on the ways in
which the analyst's interventions must often be directed to the
contextual level, or matrix, of transference (for example, the
significance of the way the patient is thinking, talking, or
behaving) before it becomes possible to address other interrelated aspects of transference (for example, the unconscious
symbolic meanings of what the patient is thinking, saying, or
enacting).

Analyzing the Shapes of Thinking and Talking

Ms. L., a college professor in her late thirties, was
referred for analysis because of chronic and intermittently paralyzing anxiety and depression. Despite the fact

that Ms. L. was highly respected by her colleagues for her teaching and research, she derived only a moderate degree of pleasure from her work. The passions in Ms. L.'s life were painting and listening to music. As a child, she had spent a great deal of her time alone in her room, drawing, reading, and listening to music. The patient said that these activities *were her life* (and continued to be).

Ms. L. had had two previous experiences in analysis. The first had lasted approximately four years, during which time the patient felt unable to think. During that initial analysis, she said that she had held a piece of hard candy between her cheek and gums during each of her analytic hours and that the analyst had interpreted this as the patient's wish to suck on his breast/penis. Ms. L. found that idea ridiculous and told the analyst so. The analyst then reportedly accused her of opposing him and the analysis at every turn. The patient viewed this interaction as paradigmatic of the tone of the entire analysis.

According to Ms. L., her second analyst became quietly enraged with her and increasingly spoke to her in a contemptuous way, finally losing his temper and accusing her of being "sadistically stubborn." Both analysts concluded that Ms. L. was unanalyzable and in both instances the analyses were ended unilaterally by the analyst.

Ms. L. began our work by saying that there was a great deal that she should fill me in on and proceeded to tell me about the emptiness and despair that consumed her life. She spoke to me as if we had been working together for years and were resuming analytic work after a weekend break. She spoke with a tone that sounded like familiarity and intimacy, but struck me as an imitation of trust. It seemed to me that this imitative trust represented an unconscious attempt to bypass the processes by which two people ordinarily develop a sense of what it is like to be with one another.

The patient made only vague references to her childhood. She presented a sketchy picture of a family consisting of a mother who was often wildly angry, a father who was emotionally remote, and a sister eight years older who seemed to have a life entirely independent of the family. One of the very few specific accounts of past experience was the patient's comment that her mother had been hospitalized each year for a period of a month or so for some medical or surgical procedure related to the mother's lifelong hypochondria.

At first, I simply listened to the flood of material, not feeling any particular pressure to interfere with the patient's efforts at telling me about herself in the way she apparently wanted to. Ms. L.'s story was filled with torment by which I ordinarily would have been quite moved. The patient conveyed a sense of such thick hopelessness that I frequently wondered why she did not kill herself. (I strongly suspected that this thought represented a wish on my part that she would kill herself.)

Days, weeks, and months went by during which I said practically nothing. (In almost every session, I wondered if I were using the idea of "analytic restraint" as a ruse for sadistic withdrawal and retaliatory exploitation of this patient who seemed to have so little use for me.) Ms. L. did not complain about my silence; rather, she seemed relieved that I was not getting her off the track of all that she needed to "fill me in on." When I did occasionally ask for a clarification or offered an interpretation, the patient gave me the requested information (usually in a very vague form) or patiently waited for me to finish my thought before continuing with her monologue. Ms. L. would repeat stories almost verbatim that she had recounted many times before. I said to her that it appeared that she had no feeling that I was listening to her and that she must feel that I remembered very little, if anything, of what she told me. Over time, I realized that this intervention, although partially correct, missed the point. Ms. L. was not talking *to me,* and therefore it did not matter that she had recounted a story many times previously. Her stories were like a child's bedtime story that can (and should) be told and retold dozens of times. The pattern of the words and images is soothing in their utterly predictable rhythm, melody, and lyrics.

Gradually, I came to realize that Ms. L. and I were not involved in the beginning of an analytic dialogue. Her words were not carriers of symbolic meaning; they were elements in a cotton wool insulation that she wove around herself in each meeting.

In retrospect, it seems to have been of critical importance that in the initial years of work I did not succumb to my own wish to establish my existence in the patient's eyes by insisting that I be recognized as an analyst. Although I had not articulated this for myself at the time, I now believe that it was essential that I neither interpreted the patient's storytelling as an act of stubbornness or resistance to the analysis, nor engaged in countertransference enactments designed to allay the feelings of isolation that I was experiencing.

As time went on I attempted to talk with Ms. L. about what I thought I understood about *the way she was talking* as opposed to that which she seemed to be talking about. For example, I told her that it seemed that she felt unbearably raw when she felt blocked from the calming experience that she found in painting and listening to music. I later added that for her, hopelessness did not seem to be an entirely bad thing; after all, it provided the incomparable peacefulness of the absence of any prospect of change. I said that I believed her when she told me that for her, there was nothing worse than being surprised. These interventions represented attempts to simply name the patient's experience without any implication that things should be otherwise and without any reference to the idea that she might feel conflicted about these aspects of her life.

In the middle of the third year of analysis, Ms. L. began to tell me how well she felt I listened. This struck me as a double-edged compliment. On the one hand, I felt that I had offered Ms. L. a medium in which she felt that she could soothe herself, but this self-soothing was something that all her life she had provided for herself through reading, listening to music, and painting. The patient's soothing herself *in my presence* was at least a step in the direction of object-related experience since none of the other self-soothing activities described by Ms. L. had ever taken place in a sustained way in the presence of another person. The self-soothing "talk" with which the patient filled the analytic hours had made it bearable for her to continue being with me. It had provided her an autistic shape so perfectly reliable and predictable that her dim awareness of me could be tolerated. This "arrangement" seemed necessary for the patient, and periodic efforts at interpretation demonstrated that this period of analysis should not and could not be rushed.

There was at the same time an unmistakable note of contempt in the patient's "complimenting" me on my fine listening ability. The unstated implication was that despite the fact that I was a good listener, what I had to say was not worth very much. The angry edge of her compliment seemed to represent a more maturely object-related dimension to the transference than had existed to this point. It seemed that Ms. L. was in this way asking me not to allow her to remain encapsulated in her sensation-dominated world even though she felt grateful to me for not having interfered with her self-soothing activities.

Viewing Ms. L.'s double-edged praise of me as an indicator of her psychological preparedness for my more actively "competing" (Tustin 1980) with her system of autistic-contiguous relationships, I decided to address much more directly than I had previously, the nature of the sensory-dominated solipsistic world in which the patient wrapped herself. I said to her that in the years that we had been working together she had both told me about and demonstrated to me the ways that she had of *not living* in the world. She had from early childhood developed the capacity to collapse into herself like a star that has imploded to the size of a ping-pong ball. Her immersion in the sensations, rhythms, and ecstasies of art and music had consumed almost every waking moment of her life outside of her work and had become substitutes for almost every other form of experience. I added that in the analysis, her storytelling served as a way of *not talking to me,* of not being in the room with me. The stories were like lullabies that she sang to herself.

The patient listened and was silent for about a minute. She then went on talking in a way that at first appeared to be a response to what I had said, but within moments revealed itself to be the beginning of the repetition of a story about a childhood event that she had recounted many times before. In the following meeting, the patient talked as usual for about 20 minutes before saying that she was furious that I was so insensitive as to repetitively tell her something she already knew. Did I

think that she was stupid? Did I really need to be so
intrusive in my comments? I said to her that it seemed
that she had not liked what I had said, but was not talking
to me about what had upset her about my comments. The
patient then returned to telling still another story about
her childhood that had the superficial appearance of
being a response to my intervention. I interrupted the
story (since there were no pauses that allowed a dialogue
to take place) and said that I thought that she had been
upset by what I had just said and that it was comforting
to her to return to a form of storytelling that served to
soothe her like a familiar lullaby. The lyrics and melody
were fully known and predictable and would never
change. The same could not be said of me and I thought
that that fact both frightened and infuriated her.

Over the succeeding weeks, the patient alternated
between railing at me about my insensitivity and resuming her storytelling. During this period, I said to Ms.
L. that I thought that she was enraged at me for having
tampered with the things most sacred to her: her feelings
about her art work and her love of music.

There then followed a period of analysis in which
the patient made no reference whatever to the events just
described. It was as if a storm had passed leaving no
evidence of its having occurred. I commented on the way
in which a segment of our recent history had been
expunged in a "1984-like way." The patient said that she
knew that she was doing that and explained that she was
an expert at that game. She told me how powerful a
weapon that ability had been in her relationship with the
man with whom she had lived for several years. He would
stew after an argument while she could "turn off the light
and immediately fall into a deep, dreamless sleep." The
next morning, it would take her a moment to figure out

why her boyfriend was not talking to her. (I was more than a little surprised to hear that she had lived with a man, but decided to accept her gift of this new information without making her acknowledge the fact that she had given something to me.)

Over the following year of analysis, Ms. L.'s "storytelling" gave way to talk that included an expanded use of metaphor. For the first time she seemed to be using language in an attempt to say something to me; there were aspects of her life that she wanted me to know about. For instance, she talked about the role that "spinning" had played in her life beginning in childhood and lasting until her early twenties. This spinning was a sensation that she could feel through her body: "It was like dizziness, but it wasn't actual dizziness." This was an extension of actual spinning that she had done as a child when she was alone. In both the physical and psychological forms of spinning she could create a state of mind in which she felt insulated not only from people, but from thoughts. She used the capacity to create this somatopsychic state during the very frequent occasions when she wanted to be alone and could not physically get away from other people. She developed the capacity to learn what she had to learn in school very quickly so that she could return to her psychological spinning while sitting in class.

In the following years of analysis, the patient's ability to talk to me waxed and waned depending upon the degree of anxiety she was experiencing. However, it was usually possible for the patient and me to identify the nature of the transference feeling that had precipitated her withdrawal into storytelling or other forms of defense against the feeling of being alive in the room with me. In this way the analytic work increasingly involved the

interpretation of the way in which shifts in the matrix of
transference were related to the emergence of specific
object-related transference thoughts and feelings (e.g.,
sexual and aggressive wishes and fears).

In summary, language was initially used by Ms. L.
not for the purpose of thinking and making herself
understood. Rather, language was used almost entirely as
a sensory medium in which the patient could wrap
herself. Speech had become the antithesis of communi-
cative discourse. The interpretation of the content of the
patient's stories proved futile. Instead, interventions were
largely descriptive of the patient's experience and did not
attempt to identify intrapsychic conflicts. (There was
very little of an integrated self capable of entering into
and maintaining the psychic tension involved in internal
conflict.) When the patient gave indirect indication of her
preparedness for a disruption of (competition with) her
reliance on autistic-contiguous forms of defensive insulation, Ms. L.'s use of language in the service of *not talking*
was interpreted.

Interpretations increasingly focused on the relationship between the context of transference (the way the
patient was thinking, feeling, talking, and so on) and the
affective content of the transference (the anxiety generated as a result of the enactment of an aspect of the
patient's internal object world on the analytic stage).[2]

---

2. In interpreting the interplay between the context and content of transference, the analyst attempts to direct the patient's attention to the moment of
substitution of one form of thinking, feeling, and behaving for another.
There is an assumption, often articulated by the analyst in his interpretation,
that the patient has experienced in the analytic situation the beginnings of
thoughts, feelings, and/or sensations that were so disturbing as to lead him
to defensively alter his way of thinking, feeling, talking, and so on. That is,
the patient alters his way of generating experience in such a way that one or

Analyzing "Dissolving" Thoughts

A 25-year-old graduate student, Mr. D., began analysis saying that he was unable to study or to work because of intense feelings of anxiety and worthlessness. He also suffered from a long-standing eating disorder of an anorectic sort. Discussion of feelings about food, dieting, exercise, and so on was conspicuously absent during the first months of analytic work. Mr. D. at times found it extremely difficult to maintain a line of thought and would find himself finishing a sentence on a topic that was unrelated to the beginning of the sentence. Over time, the patient and I came to refer to this as a form of "dissolving" psychologically. At these moments he felt as if he had almost no identity and did not feel as if he were a person who could think, much less speak his thoughts in a voice that felt like his own. Mr. D. used paranoid ideation as a way of grounding himself somewhere; at least if he were convinced that someone hated him and was plotting against him, he had some sense of a self perceiving and evaluating what was happening to him. Not surprisingly, in the course of analysis, Mr. D. slipped in and out of feelings of extreme distrust of me and feelings of being attacked by me.

In the second half of the first year of analysis, it was with great caution that the patient tentatively, and very

---

another of the dimensions of experience (the autistic-contiguous, the paranoid-schizoid, or the depressive) defensively excludes the others (see Ogden 1985, 1988, 1989a,b). This alteration in the way experience is being generated is in part perceived by the analyst through his monitoring of shifts in the countertransference. The experience of being with the patient often undergoes a subtle, but discernible change resulting from an intersubjective shift in the balance of modes contributing to the creation of transference–countertransference experience.

indirectly, broached the topic of food and eating. Unlike his uncertainty about almost every other aspect of his life, the patient held a strong conviction that his moods were powerfully shaped by the foods that he ate. Each food group was felt to have a specific impact on him. For example, sugars of all sorts including those in fruits and milk made him "manicky" and wildly anxious; fats immobilized him and made him feel lethargic, hopeless, and depressed; moderate amounts of protein and grain made him feel stable and level-headed.

It was evident how delicate a subject the topics of eating and food were for this patient and therefore I refrained from commenting on the content of the patient's ideas. I decided instead to ask the patient if he was aware of how frightened he seemed to be of my saying anything to him when he talked about food. (Even this intervention proved to be too heavily directed at phantasy content and insufficiently addressed to the way the patient was thinking.) He responded by saying that even though I had not said anything yet, he knew what I was thinking. He was sure that I, like all other doctors, viewed his ideas about the effects that food had on him as "psychotic delusions." (Both of the patient's parents were psychiatrists who openly discussed the patient's behavior using diagnostic terms and regularly interpreted the unconscious meaning of his thoughts and behavior.) Mr. D. became intensely angry at me and fearful of me at this point and vowed never again to trust me with any of his thoughts about food. I said to Mr. D. that any mention that I might make, and perhaps any thoughts that I might have about food, felt to the patient as if I were making his ideas and feelings about food a "psychological issue" and that was tantamount to my attempting to drive him crazy. I went on to say that I understood that there were few enough things in his life about which he felt that he could trust his perceptions. For me to draw into question in any way what he felt he knew about his response to food would be as basic an assault on his sanity as my calling into question the veracity of his perception that this thing is a chair or that thing is a couch.

Mr. D. was relieved by this intervention, not because it involved reassurance that painful mental content would not be addressed. (Patients are almost always angry and disappointed when the analyst unconsciously assures them that an aspect of their psychopathology will not be treated.) Rather, the patient experienced the intervention as an acknowledgment of his right and his capacity to name (and misname if he chose) his own bodily states without having this self-defining process co-opted by me.

The patient had reported that in a previous analysis, the analyst had acted as if she knew what the patient was feeling better than the patient himself did. Under circumstances when the analyst consciously or unconsciously conducts himself as if he believes that he knows the patient's experience better than the patient does, there ceases to be a recognition of the existence of two people in the consulting room; instead, only the analyst and his conception of the patient's experience remain. This almost always represents a repetition of an early childhood experience (of the patient and/or the analyst) wherein the mother unconsciously saw in her infant only the aspects of herself that she projected into him.

I view the intervention in which I discussed the patient's fear that I was driving him crazy as a necessary interpretation of the context of meaning that must precede the interpretation of psychological content (e.g., the conflicted meanings that food held for Mr. D.). The

aspect of the patient's experience that had to be addressed
before all else was the idea that his thinking was functioning in the service of an attempt to hold on to a
dissolving sense of self. His thoughts were being generated in order to preserve what little there was remaining
of his sense that he existed. The concreteness of Mr. D.'s
thinking served to make his thoughts feel more real and
less likely to be stolen or taken over by me. As the patient
looked back on this period, he said that it had felt as if his
thoughts had become "hardened" and in that state could
be more easily "held on to." He experienced all ambiguity
of meaning as extremely frightening since he would feel
as if he were "slipping and sliding over the surface of very
thin ice."

It was possible over time to understand the way in
which thinking in a concrete way represented an unconscious attempt to ward off the threat of "dissolving,"
"falling," "losing a thought," and so on. Further it was
possible to observe and to interpret the way in which this
threat arose in the context of a (maternal transference)
experience of me as someone so "adept" at interpreting
Mr. D.'s experience that only I knew what he was
thinking and feeling. Much later, the patient became
aware that he had originally chosen me as his analyst in
part because he had hoped that I would be so perceptive
as to be able to know his thoughts before he did. This
represented a wish that he might become able to feel alive
and capable of thinking and working by getting me to live
and think for him. At the same time, the patient struggled
against such wishes because of a conviction that a submission of this sort would be the end of him. He was
afraid that once such a submission had occurred, he
would never be able to recover the fragments of his own

perceptions that provided his only connection with his flimsy sense of self.

To summarize, in the fragment of analytic work discussed here, it was necessary to analyze in the transference the function of the way the patient was thinking before the content of that thought process became accessible for analysis. After an initial, poorly timed intervention, the interpretive focus was shifted to the way in which the patient's thinking served to help him preserve his fragile and ever-eroding sense of self.[3]

Analyzing Sexual Things-in-Themselves

Ms. R., a 25-year-old junior high school teacher, began analysis because of intense anxiety of a diffuse nature. She had had a severe anxiety attack while teaching and was afraid that further attacks would follow and result in her losing her job. In the initial meetings, the patient presented herself in a halting, self-conscious, and somewhat prudish manner. She was an attractive woman, but dressed and wore her hair in a way that conveyed a sense of barrenness. Ms. R. said that she had had "relationships" with men, but she was vague about this and left it

---

3. The most important of Freud's (1915b) three major theories of schizophrenia involved a similar emphasis on the patient's formation of "thing presentations" (p. 203), not for the purpose of internal communication or for the purpose of trial action, but for the purpose of using thinking (the creation of thing presentations) as an attempt to hold onto or regain a connection with the external world. In other words, schizophrenic thinking (the process of generating thing presentations) was conceived of as the patient's attempt to retain or regain his sanity.

quite unclear as to what, if any, sexual experiences she had had.

In the course of Ms. R.'s giving me an account of the people in her life who were important to her, I was struck by her sense of the brittleness of the ties that existed between people. Long-standing friendships could be destroyed if one were to say the wrong thing at the wrong time; a friend's father had had a heart attack within days of his daughter's informing him of her engagement to marry; her own father had been abruptly fired from his job after a dispute with his boss.

Several weeks into the analysis, the patient announced that it was necessary for her to discontinue analysis for financial reasons. There was no convincing evidence that financial difficulty accounted for the patient's precipitous flight. I asked her what else she thought might be involved in her decision. After reflexively saying that that was all that was involved, she admitted that she had felt increasingly hopeless about the possibility of getting anything out of analysis.

I said to her that she had made it clear in the weeks that we had been meeting that words and thoughts were deadly serious things that should never for a moment be treated as "just talk." People could be badly hurt if they were not extremely careful about what they said to others and what others said to them. She turned on the couch and looked at me in a way that reflected the fact that she was intensely interested in this subject and was surprised that I understood the enormous power of words.

Ms. R. said that in childhood she could not understand how other children could recite nursery rhymes about heads being smashed open (e.g., "Humpty Dumpty" and "Jack and Jill"), about fathers dying ("My country 'tis of thee"), and about spiders terrifying children ("Little Miss Muffet") without being as terrified as she had been. She went on to talk about the way in which she had often been deeply hurt because she had taken people at their word. If a man at a party were to tell her that he would call her, she would treat this as a solemn promise. She said that in first grade when her teacher told the class that they would have "show and tell" each morning, she became extremely anxious fearing that she would have to reveal her secrets or perhaps even take off her clothes. Moreover, she was not certain whether the teacher had said "show" or "shower."

I then said that I wondered if she felt that analysis involved revealing herself to me and that she had begun to despair that if she were not willing or able to literally bare herself to me, she would get nothing out of it. On the other hand, it would be devastatingly humiliating if she were to force herself to reveal herself to me.

The patient cried and told me that in college she had read that Freud believed that ultimately everything was sexual. She asked me if I thought that everything had a sexual meaning. I told her that that would mean that she and I would be continually engaging in "dirty talk." She agreed and said that she had no wish whatever to do that to me or for me to do that to her. This interchange led to a decrease in Ms. R's level of anxiety sufficient for her to continue in analysis.

It is not possible in this brief discussion to offer more than a schematic overview of the unfolding of the analytic process. In what follows I shall attempt to illustrate something of the movement from the analysis of the matrix of transference (concretely elaborated in the experience of talking as sexual action) to the analysis of the content of unconscious fantasy that is symbolically elaborated (as thoughts and feelings) in the transference.

In the succeeding months of analysis, the patient discussed her childhood experience in considerably greater
detail than she had previously. Ms. R said that she could
not recall ever seeing her parents argue and yet the
tension between them was so great that she would become
nauseated and develop headaches when she spent an
extended length of time with the two of them. Each
seemed to be a master of the "vicious innuendo" and
"looks that eviscerated." The patient described chronic
insomnia beginning at about age 3 or 4 that continues to
the present. She cried as she described the intense feelings
of loneliness that she felt as she lay in bed unable to sleep.

As this material was being presented, Ms. R. became increasingly anxious and developed an intensely
held conviction that I was deriving great pleasure from
the power I held over her as her analyst. She said that she
found it very difficult to listen to anything I said to her
because all she could focus on was the smugness that she
heard in my voice. As the analysis proceeded, the patient's relentless complaints about my "swelled head" and
contemptuous tone of voice began to feel increasingly
wearing and abrasive and I experienced a profound sense
of disconnectedness from her. Ms. R. seemed obsessed
with the idea that I was pushing her around and seemed
to take pleasure in rendering worthless anything I had to
say by reflexively responding with an accusation of this
sort. I commented to the patient on several occasions that
she seemed untiring in her attempt to goad me into a
verbal attack on her. I added that I thought that she must
feel that such an attack would make her feel less anxious
and lonely. Over time these developments in the transference–countertransference (as well as Ms. R.'s series of
dreams involving her watching "sweaty, foul-smelling"
street gangs wildly yelling and shooting at one another)

led me to increasingly suspect that Ms. R. had experienced the tension between her parents (and the process of talking with me) as a violent and confusing sexual/aggressive act. Words, tone of voice, innuendo, looks, and so on seemed to have been unconsciously experienced in a very concrete way as sexual parts of each of her parents (and of the two of us) being used to bash, enter into, injure, excite, tantalize, enrapture, and drive away the other. At the same time, not to be included in this form of relatedness led her to feel unbearably isolated.

In a session that occurred in this period of analysis, I made the following comment in response to the patient's again saying, "You don't have to bully me." I said that she was right, I did not *have to* talk to her in any particular way, but I thought that her experience of me as bullying meant to her that we were important enough to one another to become locked in battle. I later commented that I did not think that she could always tell what was hateful and what was loving about the bullying that she felt was going on between us. The patient, in a singularly uncharacteristic way, responded with reflective silence instead of a further round of accusation. This marked the beginning of a period of analysis where it became increasingly possible for Ms. R. to *talk about* feelings and ideas as opposed to enacting ideas and feelings in the form of talk.

It was not until the third year of analytic work that the patient began to directly discuss sexual feelings and fantasies. This followed the analysis of highly anxiety-laden transference fantasies involving the idea that I had a harem of female students and patients whom I treated in a callous and cavalier manner. With intense shame, Ms. R. told me in small bits and pieces over the course of almost a year, that from the time that she was 5 years old (and continuing to the present) she had masturbated two to three times a day. Ms. R. masturbated by holding a pillow or blanket between her legs. The central masturbatory fantasy (which had not changed over this period of twenty years) involved her being a member of a harem of women whose master ordered the women to have sex with him. The master was occasionally experienced as kind, but usually was pictured as impersonal, sadistic, and demanding absolute submission of the patient and the other women. Nonetheless, she felt "nothing but blind devotion and loyalty" to this man and to the other women. This form of compulsive masturbation and the fantasies associated with it were understood as serving a number of critically important psychological functions. At its most primitive level, this activity seemed to serve a self-soothing and self-defining function. The patient, in the face of the experience of extreme isolation from early on, had constructed a sensation-dominated form of relatedness (to an autistic shape) through which she attempted to maintain the fragile coherence of self that she had achieved.

At the same time, Ms. R. used the fantasy of the harem as a way of constructing an internal object family for herself. The patient had invented a version of the Oedipus complex that was based on the wish for integration and inclusion (albeit at the cost of personal identity and mutual recognition). Ambivalence and parricidal wishes were regressively transformed into blind devotion to an omnipotent object; rivalry and recognition of generational difference were converted into the ties between siblings and narcissistic twinship.

To conclude, in the very early stages of the analysis, talking about sex with me was experienced by the patient as equivalent to having sex with me. The analysis itself was experienced as a sexual enactment rather than as an arena in which sexual thoughts and feelings might be experienced, discussed, and understood. It was therefore essential to talk about the way in which talking was experienced as sexual enactment (i.e., to analyze the contextual level of transference) before addressing other levels of transference meaning.[4] As a result of the analysis of the heavily paranoid-schizoid contextual level of transference (talking as a sexual/aggressive event), the patient was eventually able to achieve a shift toward an increasingly depressive mode of generating experience. Her sexual anxiety did not disappear; rather, it was experienced differently. What had formerly been the experience of frightening sexual things in themselves (hurled about in the form of words) became frightening and confusing sexual and aggressive feelings and ideas that did not immediately have to be deflected through the use of concrete word barriers (in the form of defensive accusations).

Concluding Comments

The matrix of transference can be thought of as the intersubjective correlate (created in the analytic setting) of the psychic space within which the patient lives. The transference matrix

---

4. In analytic work with patients functioning in a predominantly paranoid-schizoid mode, one must keep in mind that the analyst's attempt to explore the patient's fear of talking about sex (without first analyzing the contextual level of transference) is regularly heard as a seductive and coercive inquiry into the question of why the patient is refusing to have sex with the analyst. The combination of fear and excitement that the patient experiences under such circumstances often leads to a flight from analysis or to other forms of acting out.

reflects the interplay of fundamental modes of structuring experience (the autistic-contiguous, the paranoid-schizoid, and the depressive) that together make up the distinctive quality of the experiential context within which the patient creates psychic content. This concept addresses not only the events occurring on the analytic stage, but the states of being determining the nature of the ways in which thoughts, feelings, sensations, and behavior are created, experienced, and interpreted by the patient.

The analysand does not simply speak to the analyst (or himself) *about* the ways in which he creates experience; rather, he contributes to an intersubjective construction within the analytic setting that incorporates *in its shape and design* the nature of the psychic space within which the patient lives (or fails to come to life). Invariably, the analyst unconsciously participates in the creation of the intersubjective construction within the analytic setting. It is in part through this avenue (i.e., through countertransference analysis) that the analyst gains access to the nature of the states of being comprising the matrix of the patient's internal world.

Summary

In this chapter, the background experiential states forming the matrix of transference are discussed in terms of the interplay of three modes of generating experience: the autistic-contiguous, the paranoid-schizoid, and the depressive. Portions of three analyses are discussed in an effort to clinically illustrate some of the ways in which analytic technique is shaped by an understanding of the predominant mode or modes of experience forming the context of the transference–countertransference at any given moment. The chapter focuses on the ways in which the analyst's interventions must often be directed to the contextual level, or matrix, of transference (for example, the significance of the way the patient is thinking, talking, or behaving) before it becomes possible to address other inter-related aspects of transference (for example, the unconscious symbolic meanings of what the patient is thinking, saying, or enacting).

9

Personal Isolation:
The Breakdown of Subjectivity
and Intersubjectivity

*It remains to learn in what delicate, exquisite region
of Being we shall encounter that Being which is its
own Nothingness.*
Jean-Paul Sartre, *Being and Nothingness*

In the course of the past decade, I have come to view the
concept of personal isolation as central to an understanding of
human development. My own conception of personal isolation
is based upon ideas derived from the psychoanalytic study of
autistic phenomena as well as Winnicott's conception of isolation as a necessary condition for psychological health.

Winnicott's work will be taken as a starting point for the
understanding of personal isolation as an essential facet of the
experience of being alive. I shall then attempt to describe a
primitive form of isolation that involves the disconnection of
the individual not only from the mother as object, but also
from the very fabric of the human interpersonal matrix.

The idea that there is an aspect of experience in which the individual must be insulated from being in the world has its origins in Freud's (1920) concept of the stimulus barrier (*Reizschutz*). Freud believed that the preservation of the organism is as much dependent upon the capacity not to perceive as it is upon the capacity to register internal and external stimuli: "[The organism] would be killed . . . if it were not provided with a protective shield against stimuli. It acquires the shield in this way: its outermost surface ceases to have the structure proper to living matter, becomes to some degree inorganic and thenceforward functions as a special envelope or membrane resistant to stimuli . . . By its death, the outer layer has saved all the deeper ones from a similar fate" (p. 27). In this chapter, I shall make use of concepts emanating from the psychoanalytic study of autistic phenomena to further develop the idea that the experience of being alive as a human being is safeguarded by forms of suspension of being.

Winnicott's Conceptions of Isolation

The discussion of personal isolation must begin with the study of Winnicott's seminal contributions to this area of thought. Winnicott (1963) viewed the individual as (in part) "an isolate, permanently unknown, in fact unfound" (p. 183). He believed that the isolation of the infant from the object objectively perceived is an essential experiential context for the development of a sense of realness and spontaneity of the self. The concept of isolation is an idea that evolved over the entire span of Winnicott's writing. It overlaps and is intertwined with such ideas as the holding environment, relatedness to transitional objects, the capacity to be alone, the experience of playing, and the development of the True and False Self. In the present discussion, I shall focus on what I understand to be the two principal conceptions of isolation developed by Winnicott. (Although the two "forms" of isolation that will be discussed can be understood as having a sequential, developmental relationship to one another, they must at the same time be thought of as coexisting facets or qualities of a single, dynamic phenomenon: the experience of personal isolation.)

The developmentally earlier form of isolation described by Winnicott involves the insulation of the infant from premature awareness of the separateness of self and object. This insulation is provided by the mother-as-environment as she meets the infant's need before it becomes desire (Winnicott 1945, 1951, 1952, 1956, 1971c). In so doing, there is a postponement of awareness of the separate existence of the object of desire. As importantly, the infant is protected (isolated) from the awareness of desire itself, and therefore, of the separate existence of the self. The reliability of the mother-as-environment renders her (and the infant) invisible. The non-self-reflective state of being that occurs within the context of the mother-as-environment is termed by Winnicott (1963) a state of "going on being" (p. 183). (The phrase "going on being" is particularly apt in that it names a state of aliveness without reference to either subject or object.)

The developmentally later form of isolation that Winnicott (1958a, 1962, 1963, 1968) discussed is that of relatedness to objects that are created and not found. Such objects are termed *subjective objects*. The mother-as-environment provides the infant a form of isolation from externality by means of an illusion of "omnipotence" (1963, p. 182). The mother creates this illusion by providing the breast when and in the way that it is needed and desired by the infant. Winnicott's term *omnipotence* is a bit of a misnomer since there is no experience of power over, or domination of, the object. In fact, the infant's experience of himself as powerful would reflect a breakdown

of the infant's unself-conscious illusion that the world is simply
a reflection of himself. The infant need not control the object;
the heart of this illusion is the infant's sense that the object
could not be otherwise. In this way, the infant begins to
apprehend the qualities of his own individuality as he sees
himself reflected in the world that he has "created." From an
outside observer's point of view, the mother substantiates
(gives observable, palpable form to) the infant's internal state
through the way in which she responds to him. For example,
the infant's curiosity is reflected (given observable shape) in the
mother's tone of voice, facial expressions, tempo of motion,
and so on: "The mother is looking at the baby and *what she looks
like is related to what she sees there*" (Winnicott 1967, p. 112).

The subjective object (created through this form of
interaction with the mother) is therefore both a creation of and
reflection of the evolving self. Subjective objects are internal
objects that are derived from this form of early mother-infant
interaction. Communication with subjective objects is a "cul-
de-sac communication" (Winnicott 1963, p. 184), a communication that is not addressed to external objects and therefore
entails an isolation of the self from the necessity to be
responsive to objects objectively perceived.[1] Communication
with subjective objects is (from an outsider's point of view)
"futile" (p. 184) and yet "carries all the sense of real" (p. 184).
Isolation of this sort is experientially related to a sense of
privacy as opposed to a feeling of loneliness.

In summary, Winnicott has developed conceptions of two
forms of isolation, each of which facilitates the development of

---

1. This form of isolation (relatedness to subjective objects) becomes one pole
of a dialectic that underlies the creation of transitional phenomena (Winnicott 1951, 1971a). Relatedness to subjective objects and communication with
objects objectively perceived coexist in dialectical tension in the creation of
transitional objects. Such objects are both created and discovered; the
question as to which is the case never arises.

the self and each of which paradoxically involves a disconnection from the mother as object that is achieved within the (invisible) mother-as-environment.

Autism and Multiplicity of Forms of Consciousness

Before presenting my own conception of a type of isolation more primitive than those described by Winnicott, I would like to briefly comment on the Mahlerian notion of an early phase of autism and to introduce the idea of coexisting forms of consciousness.

For decades, Margaret Mahler's (1968) conception of a normal early phase of autism followed by a "hatching" subphase represented an important organizing concept for psychoanalytic developmental theory.[2] However, there is, by now, general consensus among analytic thinkers (supported by neonatal observational studies and the application of ethological models to psychoanalysis) that the infant at birth is already a psychological entity engaged in a complex set of interpersonal interactions with the mother. There is little if any evidence to support the notion of an early stage or phase of development in which the infant exists in a cocoon-like state that is preliminary to primitive relatedness to human beings. At present, such a position seems untenable. The work of Bower (1977), Brazelton (1981), Eimas (1975), Sander (1964),

2. At the end of her life, Mahler reportedly modified her position with regard to her idea that in the earliest months of life, the infant lives in a "closed monadic system, self-sufficient in its hallucinatory wish fulfillment" (1968, p. 7), and began to integrate the findings of neonatal observational studies concerning the infant's responsiveness to his human and nonhuman environment (cf. Stern 1985).

Stern (1977), Trevarthan (1979), and many others has provided powerful evidence for the notion that from the first
moments of extrauterine life, the infant is constitutionally
equipped to perceive and enter into a reciprocal dialogue with
the mother or other caregiver.

The debate concerning the question of whether the infant
is in the beginning at one with the mother (and therefore
unaware of her separate existence and his own) or whether the
infant is capable of recognizing the difference between himself
and the other, is a more complex matter. It seems to me that
it is no longer necessary or advisable to construct our questions
about infantile experience in such a way as to force us to
choose between the notion of the infant being at one with the
mother or separate from her. Instead, if we view infantile
experience (and human experience in general) as the outcome
of a dialectical process involving multiple forms of consciousness (each coexisting with the others), it is no longer necessary
to cast our questions in terms of mutually exclusive oppositions
(Grotstein 1981, Stern 1983). The question of whether the
infant is at one with the mother or is separate from her
becomes a question of the nature of the interplay between
simultaneous experiences of at-one-ment and of separateness.
These forms of experience are not viewed as entering into a
compromise formation or a mutually diluting (averaging)
interaction; rather, the different forms of consciousness are
understood to coexist dialectically in a way that is comparable
to the relationship of conscious and unconscious experience
(see Ogden 1986, 1988). Each provides a negating and preserving context for the other. The experience of at-one-ment
does not dilute the experience of separateness any more than
the experience of consciousness dilutes unconsciousness. Each
form of consciousness maintains its own qualities that have
meaning that is in large part created by its relationship to that
which it is not.

The Sensation Matrix

As further background for the understanding of primitive isolation, I would now like to present briefly a group of concepts emanating from the psychoanalytic investigation of autistic phenomena. The primitive type of isolation that will be discussed involves an isolation of the individual in a self-generated sensation matrix (which substitutes for the interpersonal matrix). In what follows, I shall attempt to provide a vocabulary for thinking about the notion of auto-sensuous isolation.

In previous papers (Ogden 1988, 1989a,b; see also Chapters 3 and 8), I have introduced the idea that there exists a psychological organization more primitive than those addressed by Klein's (1946, 1958) concepts of the paranoid-schizoid and depressive positions. I have designated this psychological organization the *autistic-contiguous position*[3] and conceive of it as standing in dialectical tension with the paranoid-schizoid and depressive positions. It must be borne in mind that the term *autistic* is used in this context to refer to specific features of a universal mode of generating experience and not to a severe form of childhood psychopathology or its sequelae. It would be as absurd to conceive of the autistic-contiguous position as a phase of infantile autism as it would be to conceive of the paranoid-schizoid position as a phase of

3. In proposing the concept of an autistic-contiguous position, I have attempted to integrate and extend the pioneering work of Bick (1968, 1986), Meltzer (Meltzer 1986, Meltzer et al. 1975), and Tustin (1972, 1980, 1981, 1984, 1986), as well as that of Anthony (1958), Anzieu (1985), Fordham (1977), E. Gaddini (1969, 1987), R. Gaddini (1978, 1987), Grotstein (1978), Kanner (1944), S. Klein (1980), Mahler (1952, 1968), D. Rosenfeld (1984), and Searles (1960). Other conceptions of a position more primitive than the paranoid-schizoid position have been independently introduced by Bleger (1962) in Argentina and Marcelli (1983) in France.

infantile paranoid schizophrenia, or the depressive position as a universal period of childhood depression.

As discussed in Chapter 8, the autistic-contiguous position is characterized by its own distinctive form of relatedness to objects in which the object is a sensation experience (particularly at the skin surface). Such sensory experience is an experience of *being-in-sensation.* Within this sensation-dominated realm, the experience of objects is predominantly in the form of relatedness to "autistic shapes" (Tustin 1984) and "autistic objects" (Tustin 1980). Autistic shapes are "felt shapes" (Tustin 1984, p. 280) that arise from the soft touching of surfaces that make sensory impressions at our skin surface. These are not experiences of the "thingness" of an object; rather, they are the experience of the feel of the object held softly against one's skin. This shape is idiosyncratic to each of us and represents the beginnings of the experience of place. For example, the breast is not exprienced as part of the mother's body that has a particular (visually perceived) shape, softness, texture, warmth, and so on. Instead (or more accurately, in dialectical tension with the experience of the breast as a visually perceived object), the breast as autistic shape is the experience of being a place (an area of sensation of a soothing sort) that is created (for example) as the infant's cheek rests against the mother's breast. The contiguity of skin surfaces creates an idiosyncratic shape *that is the infant at that moment.* In other words, the infant's being is in this way given sensory definition and a sense of locale.

The experience of autistic objects represents quite a different sensory event from the experience of autistic shapes. Autistic objects are sensory experiences that have a quality of hardness and/or edgedness and serve to create a feeling of protectedness against nameless, formless dread. Such sensations might arise from the pressing of a stone hard into the palm of one's hand. As with autistic shapes, it is not the visually perceived thingness of the object that is experienced; rather, the experience of an autistic object is one of *being a hard shell or crust*.

The use of autistic shapes and objects is by no means a phenomenon exclusively associated with severe psychological illness. Relatedness to autistic shapes constitutes a part of normal infantile, childhood, and adult development. For example, the comfort that an infant experiences in thumb sucking is not only derived from the representational value of the thumb as stand-in for the breast; in addition, there is a dimension of thumb sucking that can be understood as involving a relationship to an autistic shape through which a sense of self-as-sensory-surface is generated.

Similarly, relationships to autistic objects represent an aspect of psychological life of healthy individuals from infancy onward. For example, "pushing oneself to one's limits" intellectually and/or physically generates a psychological state in which the individual feels fully engrossed, not only in meeting specific ego ideals, entering into competition (unconsciously phantasied as a battle), and so on; in addition, such activity often involves a dimension of relatedness to an autistic object through which one creates a palpable sensory "edge" that helps provide a sense of boundedness of self.

Relations with autistic shapes and objects are "perfect" in that they lie outside of the unpredictability of relations with human beings. Autistic shapes and objects (for example, hair twirling and biting down on the inner surface of one's cheek) are sensory experiences that can be replicated in precisely the same way whenever they are needed. These "felt shapes" and "felt objects" exist outside of time and place.

I would like to focus for illustrative purposes on rumination as a use of ideation as an autistic shape. Rumination is a form of mental activity that can be called upon instantaneously as a sensory medium in which one can immerse oneself. The repetitive thoughts are associated with a rhythmic set of "physical-mental" sensations, that is, a state of mind that has a palpable, sensory quality. The individual and the sensation-thought are one. To a large degree, there is simply a sensation-thought in the absence of a thinker. (This absence of subjectivity is akin to Bion's [1977] notion of a "thought without a thinker.") Rumination can be compared to a flaw-lessly operating machine. Nothing in the world of object relations can begin to compete with its reliability.

Primitive Isolation

With the background provided by the foregoing discussion of (1) Winnicott's conceptions of personal isolation, (2) the notion of a dialectical interplay among a multiplicity of forms of consciousness, and (3) the concept of relatedness to autistic shapes and objects, it is now possible to offer some comments on a type of isolation that involves a more radical disconnection from human beings and yet is no less life-sustaining than those forms of isolation previously described.

The isolation associated with experience of an autistic-contiguous sort involves a more thorough detachment from the world of human beings than either of the two forms of isolation described by Winnicott. Isolation of an autistic-contiguous sort involves *to some degree* the act of substituting a self-generated sensation environment for the mother-as-environment. The mental activity involved in the creation of this sensation-environment has the effect of suspending the individual somewhat precariously between "the land of the living" and "the land of the (psychologically) dead." Coming alive as a human being involves the act of being held by and within the matrix of the physical and psychological aliveness of the mother (initially the mother-as-environment and later the mother-as-object). This aspect of normal development, including the necessary isolation of the individual from premature awareness of the externality of the object (and the separateness of self and object) has been described above. What I would like to add to this conception of early development is the notion that psychological life does not unfold exclusively within the context of the mother-as-environment. I am proposing that from the beginning of psychological life (and continuing throughout life), there exists a form of experience in which the mother as psychological matrix is replaced by an autonomous sensory matrix. In replacing the environmental mother with an autonomous sensation matrix, the infant creates an essential respite from the strain (and intermittent terror[4]) inherent in the process of coming to life in the realm of living human beings.

The autistic-contiguous dimension of isolation constitutes a universal dimension of human experience and is an essential part of the overall process of coming alive as a human being. It represents a necessary resting point or sanctuary within the process of becoming (and being) human.[5] Autistic-contiguous isolation stands in contrast to the stable, impenetrable solipsism of pathological autism. The primitive isolation that I am describing represents a sensation-dominated form of insulation

---

4. Failure of the mother to provide a good enough holding environment (whether primarily the result of the inadequacy of the mother or a reflection of the hypersensitivity of the infant) is experienced by the infant as the terror of impending annihilation (Winnicott 1952). An important dimension of this feeling of terror is the sensation of falling or leaking into boundless, shapeless space (Bick 1968, D. Rosenfeld 1984).
5. Perhaps the non-REM portion of sleep (dreamless sleep devoid of both dream objects and "the dream screen" [Lewin 1950]) represents a form of being that is isolated from both the mother-as-object and the mother-as-environment.

that serves to protect the individual against the continuous strain that is an inescapable part of living in the unpredictable matrix of human object relations. It provides a temporary suspension of being alive within the mother-as-environment as opposed to a permanent negation of being or irrevocable renunciation of the maternal matrix. The capacity to suspend being in the mother-as-environment exists in dialectical tension with the capacity to tolerate the strain (and terror) of being alive in the human interpersonal context.

The suspension of the uncertainties and unpredictability of being in the realm of the human is achieved through a shift in the balance of coexisting forms of being. The living human environment is replaced by relationships with perfectly reliable sensory experiences of an autistic-contiguous sort. Such autistic-contiguous "relationships" are machine-like in their precision and therefore can be thought of as a replacement of the human world with a nonhuman one (see Searles 1960). However, the nonhuman is not synonymous with the dead; rather, nonhuman (machine-like) sensation shapes and objects provide a context that is free of the inexplicable, unpredictable ripples and gaps that are an inevitable part of the texture of living human relationships. The type of isolation I have in mind is not a form of psychological death. (Death, conceived of as inert nothingness, cannot constitute a pole of a dialectical process.) What I am attempting to describe is a suspension of life in the world of the living and the replacement of that world with an autonomous world of "perfect" sensation "relationships."

The well-timed, periodic letting go of and retrieval of the infant from this form of isolation is an essential part of the early rhythmicity of human development. In the process of letting go of the infant, the mother must allow the infant to replace her, to exclude her (to obliterate her existence both as object and as environment). Very often, one of the most difficult facets of being a mother is the pain entailed in not being allowed to be a mother. The mother must tolerate the experience of not existing for her infant without becoming overwhelmed by feelings of depression, fear, or anger. Instead, she must be able to wait while her being-as-mother is suspended (she must allow the infant his sanctuary[6]). Fain (1971) has described mothers who are unable to let go of their infants in this way. The result is a type of infantile insomnia wherein the infant can only sleep while being physically held by the mother.

It is equally important that the mother be able to "compete" (Tustin 1986) with the perfection of the infant's sensation-dominated sanctuary in her attempts to retrieve the infant and return him to the "land of the living." Such efforts at competing with autistic phenomena require considerable confidence and feelings of self-worth on the part of the mother. (See Tustin [1986] and Chapter 8, for discussions of

---

6. An analysand who had recently given birth to a healthy infant experienced a state of panic when the infant slept, fearing that he was dead. Anxiety of this type (although usually of lesser intensity) is not uncommon and often leads the mother to be unable to sleep when the infant sleeps for fear that she will awaken to find that her baby has died. We as analysts are familiar with such anxiety and have tended to understand it in terms of universal unconscious murderous wishes as well as the projection of the mother's own sense of inner deadness. It seems to me that such understandings must be supplemented by an appreciation of an additional component of the early mother–infant relationship. I have come to view such anxiety as reflecting the mother's response to her actual experience that the infant at times has been lost to her and each time has somehow been retrieved. That is, the mother has in fact experienced the loss of her infant in the course of the infant's periodic isolation of himself in his own sensory matrix and she is terrified that this experience of "near death" will be repeated (this time irreversibly).

the transference-countertransference experience of competing with the patient's relationships with autistic shapes and objects in the analytic process.)

I have come to view pathological autism as representing a failure of the mother–infant dyad to negotiate this delicate balance between being in the mother-as-environment and the suspension of that form of being. A depressed mother may mistakenly experience this form of primitive isolation as a categorical rejection of her as mother. This may set in motion a vicious cycle of mutual withdrawal; the infant's withdrawal from the mother leads her to become despondent and over-whelmed by feelings of worthlessness, which in turn leads the infant to seek deeper refuge in his auto-sensuous sanctuary. Eventually, this spiral of disconnection of mother and infant reaches a point of no return. At this juncture, there is a collapse of the normal periodicity of withdrawal into auto-sensuality and retrieval into the realm of the human. This collapse represents a psychological catastrophe of the greatest magnitude—the infant moves beyond the "gravitational pull" of human relatedness and "floats off" into a realm of impene-trable, uninterrupted nonbeing. The crossing of this "line" represents the transformation of normal auto-sensuous isola-tion into pathological autism.

Concluding Comments

In this chapter I have attempted to expand the concept of personal isolation to include a form of isolation in which the infant replaces the mother-as-environment with his own sen-sation matrix. The creation of such a self-generated sensation matrix stands in contrast to Winnicott's concept of the early illusion of at-one-ment with the mother and his concept of relations to subjective objects, since both of the types of isolation described by Winnicott are mediated by a relationship to the mother-as-environment. The type of isolation that I have described involves a more radical withdrawal from human beings; it entails a withdrawal from the mother-as-environment as well as from mother-as-object.

Withdrawal from the mother (both as object and as environment) into a world of relations to autistic shapes and objects is viewed as a feature of normal early development. Relations to autistic shapes and objects are machine-like in their reliability and in their capacity to be endlessly replicated outside of time and place. This form of experience is not conceived of as representing an early phase or stage of development prior to object relatedness; rather, it is viewed as an ongoing facet of all human experience that serves as a form of buffer against the continual strain of being alive in the world of human beings. It provides a rim of suspended being that makes bearable the uncertainty and pain of human relations. In the absence of this facet of experience (this form of not being in the human world), we are skinless and unbearably exposed. Physiologically, it is essential that one's skin be continually generating a layer of dead tissue that serves as a life-preserving outermost layer of the body. In this way (as in Freud's concept of the stimulus barrier), human life is physiologically encapsulated by death. In this chapter, I have suggested that psychological life is from the beginning similarly safeguarded by the sanctuary provided by the experience of not being in the "land of the living."

10

Questions of Analytic Theory and Practice

In this chapter, a series of questions posed by Dr. Stephen Mitchell, editor of *Psychoanalytic Dialogues: A Journal of Relational Perspectives*, provides the structure for the consideration of a wide range of analytic topics concerning analytic metapsychology, clinical theory, developmental theory, and analytic technique. Each of the questions and responses addresses different aspects of psychoanalytic theory and practice that are fundamental to the conception of the psychoanalytic process being developed in this volume and in the work that has led to it. (I am grateful to Dr. Mitchell for the thoughtfulness and creativity that are reflected in his questions.)

Practice and Technique

Mitchell: In your description of the initial analytic session (Ogden 1989a), you stress the importance of the analyst's

183

grasping and addressing himself to the patient's anxiety and dread. This idea seems quite different from the idea that it is necessary to create a feeling of hope in the initial meetings and the view that the patient is fundamentally seeking a "new beginning." How do you think about the relationship between hope and dread in the initial phases of analysis?

Ogden: It has consistently been my experience that what allows the patient to be most hopeful about the prospect of psychological change in analysis is the experience of being understood at both a conscious and an unconscious level. In the initial meeting, offering this experience does not always mean offering the patient an interpretation since it is often the case that understanding the patient involves not interpreting, not knowing too much too early.

When one does elect to communicate one's understanding in the form of an interpretation, it has seemed to me to be of central importance to attempt to help the patient talk to the analyst about what it is that is frightening him about being in the room with the analyst at that moment. It is often the case that the initial analytic meeting is the first experience in the patient's life of talking to another person in such a way that his feelings and fantasies (including his anxiety relating to the destructiveness of his anger and his love) are being named accurately and spoken about simply and directly. There is very little that can compare with the power of this experience to instill hope in the patient that he might be able to effect changes in his life that up to this point had seemed impossible.

It has been my experience that an analytic approach that avoids addressing the patient's anxiety (particularly as it relates to the negative transference) conveys to the patient a sense that the analyst is unable or unwilling to grapple with the anger and fear that the patient is experiencing in the moment. As a result, the patient may feel despairing that the analyst will be able to tolerate the aspects of himself that the patient unconsciously feels must be addressed in his analysis. In the initial meeting, the patient is, among a great many things, unconsciously attempting to assess which aspects of himself will be left untouched by the analysis as a result of the psychological difficulties brought to the situation by the analyst. The patient is, of course, correct in his assumption that it will very likely be the limitations of the analyst's capacity to analyze the transference–countertransference that will, to a very large degree, determine the effectiveness of the analytic process that will unfold.

Mitchell: You are one of the few authors writing these days who takes an essentially psychoanalytic approach to working with very disturbed patients. Do you feel that there are facets of technique in this type of analytic work that are different from those used in work with healthier patients? How do you regard the movement, even at pioneering institutions such as Chestnut Lodge, in the direction of more supportive approaches and the widespread use of medication?

Ogden: There is a considerable number of very fine analytic thinkers currently writing about the theory and practice of the psychoanalysis of severe emotional disorders. Boyer and Grotstein (through long-standing friendships) and Searles (through his writing), as well as Adler, Gabbard, Giovacchini, Kernberg, David Rosenfeld, Segal, Tustin, and Otto Will are among those authors currently writing whose work has been particularly important to my education in this area.

It has been my observation as well as that of many others (for example, Boyer, Racker, and Searles) that a principle obstacle to the analysis of severely disturbed patients is the unanalyzed experience of the analyst in the transference–countertransference. Since it is rare, indeed, that analytic training includes either the experience of supervised work with disturbed patients or a systematic scrutiny of the analyst's experience in the transference–countertransference, it is not surprising that very few clinicians are currently being adequately trained to work analytically with severely disturbed patients. It is tempting to conclude from unsuccessful work with borderline and schizophrenic patients that the patient is unanalyzable rather than considering the question of whether the analyst is properly equipped to conduct the analysis.

It is commonly held that in work with very disturbed patients, interpretation is disruptive to the patient, and as a result, one must offer such patients "supportive" therapy. (Supportive therapy is often a euphemism for a type of therapeutic relationship in which the patient is treated as an infant incapable of understanding in words the nature of the anxieties that prevent him from conducting his life in a more maturely integrated and object-related way.) Such a point of view fails to understand that one of the most integrative, and therefore "supportive," things that we have to offer a patient is the power of verbal symbols to contain and organize thoughts, feelings, and sensations and thus render them manageable by the patient. Words help bring that which has been experienced as physical objects or forces into a system of thoughts and feelings that are experienced as personal creations that stand in a particular relationship to one another. That is, symbols help create us as subjects.

It is important not to confuse interpretation with intellectualization. Verbal symbols allow one to construct an order of things that can be understood and changed. One cannot change the past, one cannot change who one's mother or father is, one cannot change the fact that specific psychological catastrophes have occurred. One can change the way in which one views, understands, and experiences these aspects of oneself. To deny a patient access to the transformative potential of symbols is to deny him the means by which he might attempt to achieve psychological change.

With regard to the question of medication, I am not opposed in principle to its use in the treatment of disturbed patients undergoing analysis. I routinely begin work with disturbed patients without the use of medication unless there are pressing reasons to do otherwise. (Such reasons include the imminent risk of suicide, violent behavior, and the patient's experience of unbearable psychological pain.) Before introducing medication, however, I must be convinced that the interpersonal relationship and symbolic constructions that are being introduced in the process of beginning analysis are not in themselves sufficient to allow the patient (1) to engage in the type of psychological work necessary for structural change and (2) to get on with the life he has managed to construct for himself to that point.

Mitchell: You argue that Schafer's (1976) "action language" is actually the language of the depressive position and that Schafer fails to grasp the paranoid-schizoid component of psychological states, which is not simply defensive but "an ongoing component of psychological development and an ongoing facet of psychological organization" (Ogden 1986, p. 84). You seem to suggest that Schafer attributes too much choice to more disturbed patients, who may very well be trapped within terrifying "states of mind" (to use Bion's phrase). Yet, unlike some other psychoanalytic authors, you suggest (Ogden 1989a, p. 38n) that there are always some qualities of the depressive position present and therefore that the patient always has some capacity for hearing interpretations (as interpretations as well as attacks, seductions, and so on). Is the assumption that even very disturbed patients can hear interpretations as interpretations fundamental to your approaching such patients in what seems to be a purely analytic mode?

Ogden: I view all human experience as representing the outcome of a dialectical interplay of the depressive, the paranoid-schizoid, and the autistic-contiguous modes of generating experience. From that point of view, psychological change is not conceptualized in terms of making the unconscious conscious or of transforming id into ego. Instead, I understand psychic change to be a reflection of a shift within the dialectical interplay of these modes such that a more generative and mutually preserving and negating interaction is created. I therefore assume that there is always an aspect of the patient, however compromised, that is capable of making symbolic sense of the interventions that the analyst is making. In other words, there is always a depressive component of experience. Nonetheless, there are times, for instance, in work with severely paranoid patients or with patients in a floridly manic state, when the individual seems to be generating experience in an almost exclusively paranoid-schizoid mode; that is, the patient is operating in a world of things-in-themselves and is little able to make use of verbal symbols or to distinguish psychic reality from consensual reality or to view his thoughts, feelings, and behaviors as his own psychic creations.

I should emphasize that although a predominance of the paranoid-schizoid dimension of experience is most obvious in extreme forms of psychopathology, I believe that compromises of the patient's ability to generate experience in a predominantly depressive mode occur in every analysis. Under such circumstances, I find that I must often rely upon "interpretation-in-action," that is, action other than that of creating verbal symbols as a medium for interpretation. What I mean by this is that my way of conducting the analysis constitutes an interpretation that can later be put into verbally symbolized form. For instance, after I ended the session, a patient stood at the door of my consulting room and continued to talk about what he had been discussing just before I ended the session. I repeated somewhat more firmly what I had said a moment or two earlier, "Our time is up." I believe that my firmly repeating, "Our time is up," represented an interpretation that was condensed in my verbal action. The interpretation was conveyed not only by the meaning of the words that I was speaking but also by the firmness and resoluteness with which I was saying them. As a result of the analytic work that preceded the events being described, the interpretation-in-action (verbal action) conveyed the following ideas: "You may have felt that you could seduce your mother into a blurring of generational boundaries through your engaging facility with words, but you have also become aware that the results of such a 'seduction' were quite frightening to you and that has left you in the position of being your mother's eternal child. Even though you would like to repeat that with me, you also are terrified that I will get drawn into it with you and that you will find no way finally to free yourself of this sexualized/infantile form of attachment to your mother and to me."

Over the past decade, I have become increasingly aware that many of the most important elements of the interpretations that I have made have taken the form of interpretation-in-action. Usually there has been some preparation for this aspect of "interpretive action," and there has always been a "decompression" of the interpretation in the weeks, months, and years that have followed the interpretation-in-action. From this perspective, the "maintenance of the frame" of psychoanalysis is not simply a reflection of rigid obsessionality on the part of the analyst, but a very important arena for communication between patient and analyst. Acting out and acting in on the part of the patient are now more widely understood to be valuable components of the analytic dialogue (and not simply a disruption of it). The task of the analyst is not to get the patient to stop the acting out or acting in, but to "fold" these communications-in-action into the analytic space. The analyst's interpretations-in-action represent one step in this process.

With very disturbed patients, the notion of interpretation-in-action and the idea of providing a holding environment become virtually synonymous concepts. When an analyst hospitalizes a psychotic patient, he is, in effect, offering an interpretation in that activity and at the same time is providing a containing structure within which the patient might attempt to reconstitute his sense of self. He is, in effect, saying (in action) to the patient that he believes that what the patient requires cannot be provided within the context of outpatient psychoanalysis alone; a more continuous and more extensive human provision is required, one that the analyst will attempt to facilitate, although he alone cannot provide it. Often something short of hospitalization may constitute an interpretation-in-action that represents the provision of a holding environment. For example, I have on occasion allowed patients in states of near panic to make use of my waiting room as a place to spend time as they chose. I have later discussed with them the meaning of the experience of spending that time in my waiting room as well as the meaning of my allowing them to make use of me in that way.

Mitchell: What role does unconscious intent play in your understanding of projective identification? In your clinical examples, you seem to be very careful to identify your interpretive hunches as your ideas and not attribute them to the patient. Yet, the theoretical assumption is that the patient induces mental content in the analyst for the purposes of communication and/or defense. In your clinical experience, does this motive come to be uncovered and recognized as an unconscious intent? Or does the presumption of induction serve more as a clinically useful strategy for generating hypotheses for relating the analyst's experience meaningfully to the patient's present and past experience?

Ogden: In the course of interpreting a transference–countertransference event that I have understood in terms of projective identification, I will sometimes say to a patient that it seems to me that he has gone to some trouble (without realizing it) to get me to experience firsthand what he is experiencing in order for me to understand what it feels like to be, for example, possessed by envy, to be eaten alive with bitterness, to be ruthlessly plundered and discarded, and so on. In putting the interpretation in this way, I am attempting to convey my (always tentative) understanding that the patient wishes to be understood and unconsciously feels that this understanding can happen only if I feel his feelings (as opposed to experiencing feelings like his feelings). The patient is convinced that anything short of my feeling his feelings would leave him utterly isolated and without hope of making even the slightest connection with me.

At the same time as I view projective identification as involving this type of unconscious intentionality (the wish to be understood and the unconsciously determined interpersonal activity associated with it), I am also viewing projective identification as "unintentional" (i.e., lacking intentionality) in the sense that projective identification constitutes an integral component of a state of being (the paranoid-schizoid position), in which there is very little sense of "I-ness." In a paranoid-schizoid mode of experience, one's thoughts and feelings are experienced as forces and objects that are simply appearing, disappearing, being evacuated, and so on. A sense that one does something for a purpose plays a very limited role in the emotional vocabulary of this state of being. One's thoughts, feelings, and behavior are characterized by a powerful sense of automaticity. It isn't that one does something without purpose; rather, one does something because one has to. The need to communicate and be understood is experienced in this way as well. Just as one may involuntarily scream when one is frightened, one must communicate one's internal state to another by any means possible, including the induction of that feeling state in the other (who is not experienced as entirely separate from oneself). Pursuing the analogy of the scream, in projective identification one unconsciously makes use of the mind and the body of the other person (in fantasy and associated actual interpersonal pressure) to create the scream that one cannot produce oneself.

Theory and Development

Mitchell: Throughout your work you have been very concerned with reification, rigidification, and other misuses of theory in a way that is reminiscent of Bion's hope that his readers would forget his books immediately upon having read them. In your account of the historical (depressive) position, you describe a sense of "I-ness" that the patient hopefully achieves through analysis, with its appreciation of perspectivism and the subjective creation of meaning (Ogden 1986). Is there a relationship between the patient's "I-ness" and your idea of the best way for clinicians to use psychoanalytic theory, including your own work, as subjective constructions built and transformed through time?

Ogden: I view psychoanalytic theory as a group of ideas that must be interpreted and filtered through the subjectivity of the analyst. Each of the major lines of thought constituting analytic theory has been developed to a considerable degree in its own language and has its own epistemology. Although there are large areas of shared assumptions and at times seemingly identical concepts within each of these lines of thought, it has seemed to me that no two lines of analytic thinking have generated identical concepts, even when the same terms (such as object relations, transference, countertransference, resistance, fantasy, instinct, and so on) are used to designate the ideas that are being discussed. When Balint, Freud, Fairbairn, Klein, Stern, Sullivan, and Winnicott refer to unconscious fantasy, each is referring to a distinctly different idea that has been developed in its own specific context and in relation to quite different bodies of clinical experience. As a result, each of these theorists and the concepts emanating from their work have meaning within the terms of their own epistemology and have particular relevance to the clinical setting in which these ideas were developed. For instance, Fairbairn's concept of internal object relations provides a particularly powerful way of understanding the phenomenology of the transference–countertransference that evolves in psychoanalytic work with schizoid patients. Kohut's work, in turn, has its own epistemology and has special applicability to the analytic understanding of the narcissistic aspects of personality.

It is easy to say that it is the analyst's obligation to become conversant with multiple epistemologies and integrate them. I think that in reality, however, the best that we can hope for is an uneasy coexistence of a multiplicity of epistemologies. Our goal is to attempt to escape the pitfalls of ideology and to learn from our awkward efforts at thinking within the context of different systems of ideas that together, in a poorly integrated way, constitute psychoanalysis. (This way of viewing analysis should not be confused with eclecticism. The latter represents a glib acceptance of a number of points of view in a way that is marked by the absence of the anguish involved in attempting to wrestle with irreconcilably different forms of understanding, each of which is indispensable.)

The understanding of psychoanalysis that I am describing places the natural science model in the position of being one of many of the epistemologies comprising psychoanalysis. In a natural science model, there is a single unifying method (the scientific method) by which the body of knowledge is expanded. In psychoanalysis we have the much more difficult task of attempting to reconcile the diversity of forms of knowledge that we have at our disposal. We must understand the history of these lines of thought, the methods by which they were developed, and the kinds of experiences that have served as organizers of this knowledge. Each epistemology is separate unto itself and at the same time stands in dialectical tension with the others. Each is slowly and sometimes painfully being transformed by the others, and, as a result, one is not dealing with a linearly expanding body of knowledge. For instance, Klein's work can be viewed as an interpretation of Freud, and Winnicott's work can be viewed as an interpretation of Klein. Moreover, since Freud's writing contains more meaning than he himself recognized, a study of Klein and Winnicott, for example, provides a necessary avenue for the development of a fuller understanding of Freud's work.

Mitchell: In your reinterpretation of various Kleinian concepts, you characterize Klein's contribution as delineating "preoedipal forms of preconception" and as depicting "instinctual modes of organizing experience." In other places you stress Winnicott's notion of a structual readiness for finding need-fulfilling objects, a notion more vague than the specificity Klein suggests. Does your approach, and the way you draw on Chomsky in your conception of "psychological deep structure"

(Ogden 1984, 1986), suggest a reinterpretation of Freud's concept of "instinct" along cognitive as opposed to energic lines? Do you find the term *instinctual experience* useful in your own thinking at this point? What does it mean to you? Do you find Klein's presumption of specific *a priori* objects useful?

Ogden: The revision or modernization of instinct theory that I have proposed represents an attempt to integrate into analytic thought some of the advances in structuralist thinking that have occurred since Freud's time. Structuralist thought (for example, the contributions of Chomsky, Levi-Strauss, and Piaget) has advanced far beyond the stages of its development that existed when Freud and Klein were developing their ideas. It therefore seemed useful to me to incorporate modern structuralist thinking, particularly Chomsky's work in the area of linguistics, in attempting to fill out what was implicit in the structuralism of Freud and Klein. My concept of psychological deep structure is simply a way of describing the existence of biologically determined templates that serve to organize the immense quantity of experiential data with which the infant/ child is flooded. It seems to me that without psychological deep structures there would not be the commonality of human personality that characterizes our species. After all, we are far more like one another in terms of our fundamental psychic organization and sets of unconscious beliefs, fears, fantasies, and the like than we are different from one another.

As early as 1949, Isaacs, in her defense of the Kleinian concept of very early fantasy activity, introduced the idea that the object (for example, the breast) is somehow inherent in the (sucking component of the libidinal) instinct. In other words, the breast as object is somehow anticipated in the oral component of the sexual instinct. In this context, the notion of the breast refers more to a sensation than to an idea. I am in agreement with Freud and the Kleinians that universal fantasies and even constellations of fantasies such as the primal scene fantasy, castration anxiety, fantasies of childhood seduction, and the Oedipus complex represent the outcome of the readiness to organize experience along predetermined lines. For example, experience of one's feces dropping into the toilet gives form to what had previously been a "preconception" (Bion 1962b), a set of meanings that are not realized until the preconception meets its realization in actual experience. The child anxiously organizes such experiences in terms of fantasies of the loss of, or damage to, important body parts, particularly the genitalia.

Structuralist thinking falls prey to the Lamarckian fallacy of positing the existence of inherited ideas (as opposed to a readiness to organize stimuli along predetermined lines) when it becomes overly specific about the contents of the fantasies that are viewed as reflections of deep structure. Fundamental childhood fantasies, such as the fantasy of eating or being eaten by the mother, have elements of what I would consider reflections of psychic deep structure; at the same time, the particular fantasy elaborated by the child incorporates the unique experience of each child with his mother.

Having said all this, I believe it is important to emphasize that we are in danger of throwing the baby out with the bathwater, as it were, when the analytic concept of instinct is understood strictly in terms of the organization of personal meaning. To do so is to ignore a good deal of the heart of Freud's insight into the nature of human beings. Freud's psychology is founded on two basic ideas: (1) the centrality of the interplay of consciousness and unconsciousness; and (2) the idea that the principal motivation for all human activity, psychopathology, cultural achievement, and so on is sexual passion and the effort to control it. From this perspective, the idea of instinctual experience is a conception of human passion as a medium through which experience is given meaning.

Human passions and the organization of personal meaning are utterly interdependent concepts. When we try to separate the two (passion and meaning), we end up with conceptions of the human being that are unduly weighted either in the direction of the conception of the individual as lived by formless energy or a conception of the individual as an attachment-seeking entity decentered from his biologically based passions.

Mitchell: In your explication of Winnicott in *The Matrix of the Mind* (Ogden 1986), you approach the paranoid-schizoid organization essentially in terms of a breakdown of "threeness," a defensive response to what Winnicott considered "environmental failure." Yet, in the *The Primitive Edge of Experience* (Ogden 1989a), you develop a view of the paranoid-schizoid position as a perpetual, refreshing, and generative component of all experience. Do you feel there is an inherent rhythmicity to experience that naturally returns us to the purity and clarity of the paranoid-schizoid position or that such a return is always a defensive response to danger or failure?

Ogden: The question of the relationship of the paranoid-schizoid position to other aspects of experience is a very interesting one. As I have discussed, I believe that it is essential that we view these positions or states of being as coexisting dialectically. From that point of view, one deemphasizes the purely sequential or even defensive nature of these positions or states. Although Klein introduced the concept of the positions as a way of moving beyond the notion of a phase or stage, I think that she did not fully appreciate the importance of her contribution. She very often lapsed into treating these positions as developmental phases and on those occasions ran into considerable theoretical difficulty. One of the places where she has been most criticized is her insistence on associating the paranoid-schizoid position with the first three months of life and the depressive position with the second three months of life. In so doing, she has failed to recognize that the concept of position represents a significant theoretical advance over that of the concept of developmental stage.

The relationship between positions is not fundamentally a sequential or even a hierarchical one. Rather, positions are dialectically related just as the concepts of the conscious mind and the unconscious mind make no sense except when viewed as standing in a dialectical, mutually creating, negating, and preserving relation to one another. For example, I do not think of the depressive position as following the paranoid-schizoid position, but as existing from the beginning as an element of experience. This is not to say that the infant at birth perceives himself and his mother as whole and separate objects. I would put it this way: even at the very beginning of life the infant has some rudimentary sense of otherness that he bumps up against. At the same time, there is an aspect of consciousness in which the infant and other are at one. These understandings do not represent contradictory statements. Instead, they represent attempts to describe the coexistence of multiple states of consciousness. (When I speak of consciousness here, I am not referring to the capacity for reflective self-awareness, which becomes a quality of consciousness much later in life.)

I would like to return now to the question of whether the paranoid-schizoid position represents a breakdown of "three-ness" and in that sense represents a defensive response to "environmental failure." I think that I would put it differently from the way I did in *The Matrix of the Mind*. I think that a more accurate statement of this idea would be that environmental failure would lead to a shift in the dialectical interplay of the autistic-contiguous, paranoid-schizoid, and depressive positions. When there is a breakdown of functioning of the mother–infant unit, the role of the mother as provider of a buffer against feelings of helplessness in a world of not-me objects must be taken over by the infant himself. In other words, what had been, to a large extent, an intersubjective and interpersonal form of defense or illusion must become increasingly an intrapsychic act of self-defense on the part of the infant. The infant protects himself through the use of increased reliance on omnipotent forms of thinking as opposed to relying on interpersonally created states of illusion. What had been previously predominantly an experience with the (invisible) mother-as-environment has now become the experience of the mother-as-object (against whom the infant must at times protect himself).

The explanation that I have just given of the relationship of the paranoid-schizoid position to environmental failure (in a Winnicottian sense) is a good example of a place where I sense that my efforts at creating an "integrated" analytic theory stretch both the Kleinian and the Winnicottian metapsychologies to their breaking points. The two lines of analytic thought can be related to one another as I have just attempted to do, but the fit is by no means a seamless one.

Mitchell: In your reworking of preoedipal and oedipal development (Ogden 1987, 1989a,c), you tend to assign the father's role largely to the oedipal phase and attribute the experience of maleness early on to the mother's internal paternal objects and masculine identifications. How do you think of the role of the father as a real person during the preoedipal phase? Do you think the father also may serve as a subjective object, omnipotently controlled, before he is experienced as a fully external object?

Ogden: I believe that an important part of early development involves the establishment of the recognition of sexual difference, generational difference, and role difference within the family. An important corollary to this statement is the idea that the mother must be able to carry within her the internal object father and the father must be able to carry within him the internal object mother. As a result, mothering is provided both by the father and by the mother just as the mother in the "transitional oedipal period" (Ogden 1987, 1989a) serves as psychic father as well as mother.

It is as essential that the father be able to serve as a subjective object as it is for the mother to be able to play this role. I believe, however, that one goes too far if one simply says that mother and father are interchangeable. The father's version of what it is to be a subjective object is different from that of the mother. From the mother's point of view, the father never gets it quite right (and usually the father consciously or unconsciously concurs). I believe that this is the way it must be since I view this asymmetry as the experiential correlate of the idea that the father can never completely be the mother, nor should he be. The subjective object provided by the father is always "a little off." Paradoxically, the infant, the mother, and the father are all unconsciously aware that there is a distinct individuality to the father that is reflected in his form of provision of the subjective object. I believe that development has to be a little askew in this way, never perfectly symmetrical so that there are always edges against which to push off. Of course, I am describing this set of early experiences from the point of view of the family in which the mother is the primary caregiver. Under circumstances where the father is the primary caregiver I would view the situation as being reversed, with the mother providing a subjective object that is "a little off."

I see no reason why it should be essential for the mother to be the primary caregiver, nor do I believe it to be necessary for the mother to represent the component of the parental pair that is identified with "softness" and receptivity. I do believe, however, that difference is necessary for the infant to develop a conception of the complementarity between the sexes, a conception of the penis and the vagina as complementary to one another in the primal scene. Through this recognition, one must painfully come to grips with the idea that one is either male or female and not both. Involved in this recognition of difference and complementarity is the renunciation of an aspect of primitive omnipotence. The narcissistic wounds involved in the recognition of sexual difference and generational difference are essential aspects of the elaboration of the depressive position and the location of oneself in the world of consensual reality.

Mitchell: In your description of preoedipal and oedipal development, you seem to see as most fundamental not the unfolding of component psychosexual instincts themselves but the transition in object relatedness from subjective omnipotence over objects to an experience of the other's externality. Do you see this reinterpretaton, which seems to reverse the means/ends relationship of sexuality and object relations, as basically different from classical developmental theory or as merely an elaboration?

Ogden: Your question is an interesting one because it underlines for me the fact that I do not view the relationship of sexuality and object relations as having a means/end or a cause-and-effect relationship to one another. I do not view one as primary and the other as secondary. I would neither subscribe to the Fairbairnian view that sexuality is merely a type of object relatedness nor to a view (often attributed to Freud) that the object is merely the avenue through which drive tension is discharged. (Freud's view of the relationship between object relations and sexuality is, in fact, much more complex than that of the simple drive discharge model.)

Rather, I view object relatedness and sexuality as inextricable aspects of one another. Both are always qualities of human experience. It is impossible to say anything about one of these aspects of human experience without reference to the other. Therefore, it would seem inaccurate to me to say that the transition from relatedness to subjective objects to relatedness to the externality of objects is more fundamental than, or a means to achieve, the elaboration of one's sexuality.

In the papers that I have written on preoedipal and oedipal development, I have attempted to offer a way of conceptualizing the ways in which it is necessary for the child to develop a "transitional oedipal" object relationship with the mother, that is, a relationship with the preoedipal mother and oedipal father (in the mother) at the same time without being confronted by the question of which is which. This form of relationship with the other (who is and is not yet fully appreciated as the other) is part of the process by which we come to experience ourselves as being alive sexually in an increasingly complex way.

I realize as I discuss these ideas with you that I do not view my perspective as an alternative to the classical notion of sequential, phasic sexual development, nor do I see it simply as an elaboration of classical theory. Rather, I would view my thinking as a reflection of ideas emanating from a stage of development of the analytic dialogue quite different from that which served as the context for the development and elaboration of Freud's thinking on this matter. The contributions of Balint, Bion, Fairbairn, Klein, Lacan, Sullivan, Tustin, and Winnicott (to name only a few) have altered significantly the nature (as well as the content) of analytic thinking, and it is from this order of things (soon to be overcome by the evolving analytic dialogue) that my ideas have taken shape.

References

Alexander, F., and French, T. (1946). The principle of corrective emotional experience. In *Psychoanalytic Therapy: Principles and Applications*, pp. 66–70. New York: Ronald Press.

Anthony, J. (1958). An experimental approach to the psychopathology of childhood: autism. *British Journal of Medical Psychology* 31:211–225.

Anzieu, D. (1985). *The Skin Ego*. Madison, CT: International Universities Press.

Arlow, J., and Brenner, C. (1964). *Psychoanalytic Concepts and the Structural Theory*. New York: International Universities Press.

Atwood, G., and Stolorow, R. (1984). *Structures of Subjectivity: Explorations in Psychoanalytic Phenomenology*. Hillsdale, NJ: Analytic Press.

Balint, M. (1968). *The Basic Fault*. London: Tavistock.

Bibring, E. (1947). The so-called English school of psychoanalysis. *Psychoanalytic Quarterly* 16:69–93.

Bick, E. (1968). The experience of the skin in early object relations. *International Journal of Psycho-Analysis* 49:484–486.

———— (1986). Further considerations on the function of the skin in early object relations. *British Journal of Psychotherapy* 2:292–299.

Bion, W. R. (1952). Group dynamics: a review. In *Experiences in Groups,* pp. 141–192. New York: Basic Books, 1959.

——— (1959). Attacks on linking. *International Journal of Psycho-Analysis* 40:308–315.

——— (1962a). *Learning from Experience.* New York: Basic Books.

——— (1962b). A theory of thinking. In *Second Thoughts,* pp. 110–119. New York: Jason Aronson, 1967.

——— (1963). *Elements of Psycho-Analysis.* In *Seven Servants.* New York: Jason Aronson, 1977.

——— (1967). On arrogance. In *Second Thoughts,* pp. 86–92. New York: Jason Aronson.

——— (1977). Unpublished presentation at Children's Hospital, San Francisco, CA.

Blechner, M. (1992). Working in the countertransference. *Psychoanalytic Dialogues: A Journal of Relational Perspectives* 2:161–179.

Bleger, J. (1962). Modalidades de la relacion objectal. *Revisita de Psicoanálisis* 19:1–2.

Bollas, C. (1987). *The Shadow of the Object: Psychoanalysis of the Unthought Known.* New York: Columbia University Press.

Bower, T. G. R. (1977). The object in the world of the infant. *Scientific American* 225:30–48.

Boyer, L. B. (1961). Provisional evaluation of psycho-analysis with few parameters in the treatment of schizophrenia. *International Journal of Psycho-Analysis* 42:389–403.

——— (1983). *The Regressed Patient.* New York: Jason Aronson.

——— (1988). Thinking of the interview as if it were a dream. *Contemporary Psychoanalysis* 24:275–281.

——— (1992). Roles played by music as revealed during counter-transference facilitated transference regression. *International Journal of Psycho-Analysis* 73:55–70.

——— (1993). Countertransference: brief history and clinical issues with regressed patients. In *Master Clinicians on Treating the Regressed Patient,* vol. 2, ed. L. B. Boyer, and P. L. Giovacchini, pp. 1–22. Northvale, NJ: Jason Aronson.

Brazelton, T. B. (1981). *On Becoming a Family: The Growth of Attachment.* New York: Delta/Seymour Lawrence.

Buber, M. (1970). *I and Thou,* trans. W. Kaufmann. New York: Scribners.

Casement, P. (1982). Some pressures on the analyst for physical contact during the reliving of an early trauma. *International Review of Psycho-Analysis* 9:279–286.

Coltart, N. (1986). "Slouching towards Bethlehem" . . . or thinking the unthinkable in psychoanalysis. In *British School of Psychoanalysis: The Independent Tradition,* ed. G. Kohon, pp. 185–199. New Haven, CT: Yale University Press.

Eimas, P. (1975). Speech perception in early infancy. In *Infant Perception: From Sensation to Cognition,* vol. 2, ed. L. B. Cohen and P. Salapatek, pp. 193–228. New York: Academic Press.

Eliot, T. S. (1919). Tradition and individual talent. In *Selected Essays,* pp. 3–11. New York: Harcourt, Brace and World, 1960.

Erikson, E. (1950). *Childhood and Society.* New York: Norton.

Etchegoyen, R. H. (1991). *The Fundamentals of Psychoanalytic Technique.* London: Karnac.

Fain, M. (1971). Prélude à la vie fantasmatique. *Revue Française Psychanalyse* 35:292–364.

Fairbairn, W. R. D. (1952). *An Object Relations Theory of the Personality.* New York: Basic Books.

Federn, P. (1952). *Ego Psychology and the Psychoses.* New York: Basic Books.

Ferenczi, S. (1921). The further development of an "active therapy" in psychoanalysis. In *Further Contributions to the Theory and Technique of Psychoanalysis,* trans. J. Suttie, pp. 198–217. New York: Brunner Mazel, 1980.

Fordham, M. (1977). *Autism and the Self.* London: Heinemann.

Freud, S. (1893–1895). Studies on hysteria. *Standard Edition* 2.

_____ (1900). The interpretation of dreams. *Standard Edition* 4/5.

_____ (1909). Notes upon a case of obsessional neurosis. *Standard Edition* 10.

_____ (1911). Formulations on the two principles of mental functioning. *Standard Edition* 12.

_____ (1915a). Instincts and their vicissitudes. _Standard Edition_ 14.

_____ (1915b). The unconscious. _Standard Edition_ 14.

_____ (1916-1917). Introductory lectures on psycho-analysis. XVIII: Fixation to traumas—the unconscious. _Standard Edition_ 16.

_____ (1917). A difficulty in the path of psycho-analysis. _Standard Edition_ 17.

_____ (1920). Beyond the pleasure principle. _Standard Edition_ 18.

_____ (1923). The ego and the id. _Standard Edition_ 19.

_____ (1925a). A note upon the "mystic writing-pad." _Standard Edition_ 19.

_____ (1925b). Negation. _Standard Edition_ 19.

_____ (1926a). Inhibitions, symptoms and anxiety. _Standard Edition_ 20.

_____ (1926b). On the question of lay analysis. _Standard Edition_ 20.

_____ (1927). Fetishism. _Standard Edition_ 21.

_____ (1930). Civilization and its discontents. _Standard Edition_ 21.

_____ (1933). New introductory lectures on psycho-analysis. XXXI: The dissection of the psychical personality. _Standard Edition_ 22.

_____ (1940). An outline of psycho-analysis. _Standard Edition_ 23.

Gabbard, G. (1991). Technical approaches to transference hate in the analysis of borderline patients. _International Journal of Psycho-Analysis_ 72:625-639.

Gaddini, E. (1969). On imitation. _International Journal of Psycho-Analysis_ 50:475-484.

_____ (1982). Early defensive phantasies and the psychoanalytic process. In _A Psychoanalytic Theory of Infantile Experience: Conceptual and Clinical Reflections,_ ed. A. Limentani, pp. 142-153. London: Routledge, 1992.

_____ (1987). Notes on the mind-body question. _International Journal of Psycho-Analysis_ 68:315-330.

Gaddini, R. (1978). Transitional object origins and the psychosomatic symptom. In _Between Reality and Fantasy,_ ed. S. E. Grolnick, L. Barkin, and W. Munsterberger, pp. 109-131. New York: Jason Aronson.

_____ (1987). Early care and the roots of internalization. _International Review of Psycho-Analysis_ 14:321-334.

Giovacchini, P. (1979). *Treatment of Primitive Mental States.* New York: Jason Aronson.

Green, A. (1975). The analyst, symbolization and absence in the analytic setting (On changes in analytic practice and analytic experience). *International Journal of Psycho-Analysis* 56:1–22.

Grinberg, L. (1962). On a specific aspect of countertransference due to the patient's projective identification. *International Journal of Psycho-Analysis* 43:436–440.

Grossman, W. (1982). The self as fantasy: fantasy as theory. *Journal of the American Psychoanalytic Association* 30:919–938.

Grotstein, J. S. (1978). Inner space: its dimensions and its coordinates. *International Journal of Psycho-Analysis* 59:55–61.

_____ (1981). *Splitting and Projective Identification.* New York: Jason Aronson.

_____ (1987). *Schizophrenia as a disorder of self-regulation and interactional regulation.* Presented at the Boyer House Foundation Conference: The Regressed Patient, San Francisco, CA, March 21, 1987.

Grunberger, B. (1971). *Narcissism: Psychoanalytic Essays,* trans. J. S. Diamanti. Madison, CT: International Universities Press.

Guntrip, H. (1969). *Schizoid Phenomena, Object-Relations, and the Self.* New York: International Universities Press.

Habermas, J. (1968). *Knowledge and Human Interests,* trans. J. Shapiro. Boston, MA: Beacon Press, 1971.

Hartmann, H. (1950). Comments on the psychoanalytic theory of the ego. *Psychoanalytic Study of the Child* 5:74–96. New York: International Universities Press.

Hartmann, H., Kris, E., and Loewenstein, R. (1946). Comments on the formation of psychic structure. *Psychoanalytic Study of the Child* 2:11–38. New York: International Universities Press.

Hegel, G. W. F. (1807). *Phenomenology of Spirit,* trans. A. V. Miller. London: Oxford University Press, 1977.

Heimann, P. (1950). On counter-transference. *International Journal of Psycho-Analysis* 31:81–84.

Hoffman, I. (1992). Some practical implications of a social-constructivist view of the psychoanalytic situation. *Psychoanalytic Dialogues: A Journal of Relational Perspectives* 2:287–304.

Hyppolite, J. (1956). A spoken commentary on Freud's *Verneinung*. In *The Seminar of Jacques Lacan. Book I: Freud's Papers on Technique, 1953-54,* trans. J. Forrester, pp. 289-297. New York: Norton, 1988.

Isaacs, S. (1949). The nature and function of phantasy. In *Developments in Psycho-Analysis,* ed. M. Klein, P. Heimann, S. Isaacs, and J. Rivière, pp. 67-121. London: Hogarth Press, 1952.

Jacobs, T. (1991). *The Use of the Self: Countertransference and Communication in the Analytic Setting.* Madison, CT: International Universities Press.

Jacobson, E. (1964). *The Self and the Object World.* New York: International Universities Press.

Joseph, B. (1982). Addiction to near death. *International Journal of Psycho-Analysis* 63:449-456.

_____ (1985). Transference: the total situation. *International Journal of Psycho-Analysis* 66:447-454.

_____ (1987). Projective identification: some clinical aspects. In *Melanie Klein Today, Vol. 1: Mainly Theory,* ed. E. Spillius, pp. 138-150. New York: Routledge, 1988.

Kanner, L. (1944). Early infantile autism. *Journal of Pediatrics* 25:211-217.

Kernberg, O. (1976). *Object Relations Theory and Clinical Psychoanalysis.* New York: Jason Aronson.

_____ (1985). *Internal World and External Reality.* Northvale, NJ: Jason Aronson.

_____ (1987). Projection, projective identification: developmental, clinical. *Journal of the American Psychoanalytic Association* 35:795-820.

Khan, M. M. R. (1964). *The Privacy of the Self.* New York: International Universities Press.

Klauber, J. (1976). Elements of the psychoanalytic relationship and their therapeutic implications. In *The British School of Psychoanalysis: The Independent Tradition,* ed. G. Kohon, pp. 200-213. New Haven, CT: Yale University Press, 1986.

Klein, M. (1932). The effect of early anxiety situations on the sexual development of the girl. In *The Psycho-Analysis of Children,* pp.

268-325. New York: Humanities Press, 1969.

_____ (1935). A contribution to the psychogenesis of manic-depressive states. In *Contributions to Psycho-Analysis, 1921-1945*, pp. 282-311. London: Hogarth Press, 1968.

_____ (1946). Notes on some schizoid mechanisms. In *Envy and Gratitude and Other Works, 1946-1963*, pp. 1-24. New York: Delacorte, 1975.

_____ (1948). On the theory of anxiety and guilt. In *Envy and Gratitude and Other Works, 1946-1963*, pp. 25-42. New York: Delacorte, 1975.

_____ (1952a). Some theoretical conclusions regarding the emotional life of the infant. In *Envy and Gratitude and Other Works, 1946-1963*, pp. 61-93. New York: Delacorte, 1975.

_____ (1952b). The origins of transference. In *Envy and Gratitude and Other Works, 1946-1963*, pp. 48-56. New York: Delacorte, 1975.

_____ (1952c). Mutual influences in the development of ego and id. In *Envy and Gratitude and Other Works, 1946-1963*, pp. 57-60. New York: Delacorte, 1975.

_____ (1955). On identification. In *Envy and Gratitude and Other Works, 1946-1963*, pp. 141-175. New York: Delacorte, 1975.

_____ (1957). Envy and gratitude. In *Envy and Gratitude and Other Works, 1946-1963*, pp. 176-235. New York: Delacorte, 1975.

_____ (1958). On the development of mental functioning. In *Envy and Gratitude and Other Works, 1946-1963*, pp. 236-246. New York: Delacorte, 1975.

Klein, S. (1980). Autistic phenomena in neurotic patients. *International Journal of Psycho-Analysis* 61:395-401.

Kohut, H. (1971). *The Analysis of the Self.* New York: International Universities Press.

_____ (1977). *The Restoration of the Self.* New York: International Universities Press.

Kojève, A. (1934-1935). *Introduction to the Reading of Hegel*, trans. J. H. Nichols. Ithaca, NY: Cornell University Press, 1969.

Kris, E. (1950). *Psychoanalytic Explorations in Art.* New York: International Universities Press.

210

References

Kundera, M. (1984). *The Unbearable Lightness of Being,* trans. M. H. Hein. New York: Harper and Row.

Lacan, J. (1951). Intervention sur le transfert. In *Écrits,* pp. 215–226. Paris: Seuil, 1966.

––––– (1953). The function and field of speech and language in psycho-analysis. In *Écrits: A Selection,* trans. A. Sheridan, pp. 30–113. New York: Norton, 1977.

––––– (1954–1955). *The Seminar of Jacques Lacan. Book II: The Ego in Freud's Theory and in the Technique of Psychoanalysis, 1954–1955,* trans. S. Tomascelli. New York: Norton, 1988.

––––– (1957). On a question preliminary to any possible treatment of psychosis. In *Écrits: A Selection,* trans. A. Sheridan, pp. 179–225. New York: Norton, 1977.

––––– (1966a). The agency of the letter in the unconscious or reason since Freud. *Écrits: A Selection,* trans. A. Sheridan, pp. 146–178. New York: Norton, 1977.

––––– (1966b). Position de l'inconscient. In *Écrits,* pp. 829–850. Paris: Seuil, 1966.

Langs, R. (1978). *The Listening Process.* New York: Jason Aronson.

Laplanche, J., and Pontalis, J-B. (1967). *The Language of Psycho-Analysis,* trans. D. Nicholson-Smith. New York: Norton, 1973.

Lewin, B. (1950). *The Psychoanalysis of Elation.* New York: Psychoanalytic Quarterly Press.

Lichtenstein, H. (1963). The dilemma of human identity: notes on self-transformation, self-objectivation, and metamorphosis. *Journal of the American Psychoanalytic Association* 11:173–223.

Little, M. (1951). Counter-transference and the patient's response to it. *International Journal of Psycho-Analysis* 32:32–40.

––––– (1960). On basic unity. *International Journal of Psycho-Analysis* 41:377–384.

Loewald, H. (1960). On the therapeutic action of psychoanalysis. *International Journal of Psycho-Analysis* 41:16–33.

––––– (1980). *Papers on Psychoanalysis.* New Haven, CT: Yale University Press.

Loewenstein, R. (1967). Defensive organization and adaptive ego functions. *Journal of the American Psychoanalytic Association* 15:795–809.

Mahler, M. (1952). On childhood psychoses and schizophrenia: autistic and symbiotic infantile psychoses. *Psychoanalytic Study of the Child* 7:286–305. New York: International Universities Press.

––––– (1968). *On Human Symbiosis and the Vicissitudes of Individuation*, vol. 1. New York: International Universities Press.

Marcelli, D. (1983). La position autistique. Hypothèses psycho-pathologiques et ontogénétiques. *Psychiatrie Enfant* 24:5–55.

Marcuse, H. (1960). Preface: a note on dialectic. In *Reason and Revolution: Hegel and the Rise of Social Theory*, pp. vii–xiv. Boston: Beacon Press.

McDougall, J. (1974). The psychosoma and the psychoanalytic process. *International Review of Psycho-Analysis* 1:437–459.

––––– (1978). Countertransference and primitive communication. In *Plea for a Measure of Abnormality*, pp. 247–298. New York: International Universities Press.

McLaughlin, J. (1991). Clinical and theoretical aspects of enactment. *Journal of the American Psychoanalytic Association* 39:595–614.

Meltzer, D. (1966). The relation of anal masturbation to projective identification. *International Journal of Psycho-Analysis* 47:335–342.

––––– (1975). Adhesive identification. *Contemporary Psychoanalysis* 11:289–310.

––––– (1978). *The Kleinian Development. Part III. The Clinical Significance of the Work of Bion.* Perthshire, Scotland: Clunie Press.

––––– (1986). Discussion of Esther Bick's paper: "Further considerations on the function of the skin in early object relations." *British Journal of Psychotherapy* 2:300–301.

Meltzer, D., Bremner, J., Hoxter, S., et al. (1975). *Explorations in Autism.* Perthshire, Scotland: Clunie Press.

Milner, M. (1969). *The Hands of the Living God.* London: Hogarth.

Mitchell, S. (1988). *Relational Concepts in Psychoanalysis: An Integration.* Cambridge, MA: Harvard University Press.

––––– (1991). Contemporary perspectives on self: toward an integration. *Psychoanalytic Dialogues: A Journal of Relational Perspectives* 1:121–147.

––––– (1993). *Hope and Dread in Psychoanalysis.* New York: Basic Books.

Modell, A. (1976). "The holding environment" and the therapeutic action of psychoanalysis. *Journal of the American Psychoanalytic Association* 24:285–308.

Money-Kyrle, R. (1956). Normal counter-transference and some of its deviations. *International Journal of Psycho-Analysis* 37:360–366.

Ogden, T. (1978a). A developmental view of identifications resulting from maternal impingements. *International Journal of Psycho-Analytic Psychotherapy* 7:486–507.

_____ (1978b). A reply to Dr. Ornston's discussion of "A developmental view of identifications resulting from maternal impingements." *International Journal of Psycho-Analytic Psychotherapy* 7:528–532.

_____ (1979). On projective identification. *International Journal of Psycho-Analysis* 60:357–373.

_____ (1980). On the nature of schizophrenic conflict. *International Journal of Psycho-Analysis* 61:513–533.

_____ (1981). Projective identification and psychiatric hospital treatment. *Bulletin of the Menninger Clinic* 45:317–333.

_____ (1982a). *Projective Identification and Psychotherapeutic Technique.* New York: Jason Aronson.

_____ (1982b). Treatment of the schizophrenic state of non-experience. In *Technical Factors in the Treatment of the Severely Disturbed Patient,* ed. L. B. Boyer and P. L. Giovacchini, pp. 217–260. New York: Jason Aronson.

_____ (1984). Instinct, phantasy and psychological deep structure: a reinterpretation of aspects of the work of Melanie Klein. *Contemporary Psychoanalysis* 20:500–525.

_____ (1985). On potential space. *International Journal of Psycho-Analysis* 66:129–141.

_____ (1986). *The Matrix of the Mind: Object Relations and the Psychoanalytic Dialogue.* Northvale, NJ: Jason Aronson.

_____ (1987). The transitional oedipal relationship in female development. *International Journal of Psycho-Analysis* 68:485–498.

_____ (1988). On the dialectical structure of experience: some clinical and theoretical implications. *Contemporary Psychoanalysis* 24:17–45.

_____ (1989a). *The Primitive Edge of Experience*. Northvale, NJ: Jason Aronson.

_____ (1989b). On the concept of an autistic-contiguous position. *International Journal of Psycho-Analysis* 70:127–140.

_____ (1989c). The threshold of the male Oedipus complex. *Bulletin of the Menninger Clinic* 53:394–413.

Ondaatje, M. (1987). *In the Skin of the Lion*. New York: Knopf.

O'Shaughnessy, E. (1983). Words and working through. *International Journal of Psycho-Analysis* 64:281–290.

Pick, I. (1985). Working through in the counter-transference. In *Melanie Klein Today, Vol. 2: Mainly Practice*, ed. E. Spillius, pp. 34–47. London: Routledge, 1988.

Pontalis, J.-B. (1972). Between the dream as object and the dream-text. In *Frontiers in Psycho-Analysis: Between the Dream and Psychic Pain*, pp. 23–55. New York: International Universities Press, 1981.

Puig, M. (1980). *Eternal Curse on the Reader of these Pages*. New York: Random House, 1982.

Racker, H. (1952). Observaciones sobra la contratransferencia somo instrumento técnico; communicación preliminar. *Revisita de Psicoanálisis* 9:342–354.

_____ (1968). *Transference and Countertransference*. New York: International Universities Press.

Reider, N. (1953). A type of transference to institutions. *Bulletin of the Menninger Clinic* 17:58–63.

Ricoeur, P. (1970). *Freud and Philosophy: An Essay on Interpretation*, trans. D. Savage. New Haven, CT: Yale University Press.

Rosenfeld, D. (1984). Hypochondrias, somatic delusion, and body schema in psychoanalytic practice. *International Journal of Psycho-Analysis* 65:377–388.

_____ (1992). *The Psychotic: Aspects of the Personality*. London: Karnac.

Rosenfeld, H. (1952). Notes on the psycho-analysis of the superego conflict of an acute schizophrenic patient. *International Journal of Psycho-Analysis* 33:111–131.

_____ (1965). *Psychotic States: A Psycho-Analytic Approach*. New York: International Universities Press.

_____ (1971). Contribution to the psychopathology of psychotic states: the importance of projective identification in the ego structure and the object relations of the psychotic patient. In _Problems of Psychosis_, ed. P. Doucet and C. Laurin, pp. 115–128. Amsterdam: Excerpta Medica.

_____ (1978). Notes on the psychopathology and psychoanalytic treatment of some borderline patients. _International Journal of Psycho-Analysis_ 59:215–221.

_____ (1987). _Impasse and Interpretation_. London: Tavistock.

Sander, L. (1964). Adaptive relations in early mother-child interactions. _Journal of the American Academy of Child Psychiatry_ 3:231–264.

Sandler, J. (1976). Countertransference and role responsiveness. _International Review of Psycho-Analysis_ 3:43–47.

_____ (1987). _From Safety to Superego_. New York: Guilford.

Sartre, J.-P. (1943). _Being and Nothingness_, trans. H. Barnes. New York: Philosophical Library, 1956.

Schafer, R. (1976). _A New Language for Psychoanalysis_. New Haven, CT: Yale University Press.

_____ (1978). _Language and Insight_. New Haven, CT: Yale University Press.

Scharff, J. (1992). _Projective and Introjective Identification and the Use of the Therapist's Self_. Northvale, NJ: Jason Aronson.

Searles, H. (1960). _The Nonhuman Environment in Normal Development and in Schizophrenia_. New York: International Universities Press.

_____ (1979). _Countertransference and Related Subjects_. New York: International Universities Press.

Segal, H. (1957). Notes on symbol formation. _International Journal of Psycho-Analysis_ 38:391–397.

_____ (1981). _The Work of Hanna Segal: A Kleinian Approach to Clinical Practice_. New York: Jason Aronson.

Spence, D. (1987). Turning happenings into meanings: the central role of the self. In _The Book of the Self: Person, Pretext and Process_, ed. P. Young-Eisendrath and J. Hall, pp. 131–150. New York: New York University Press, 1987.

Spruiell, V. (1981). The self and the ego. *Psychoanalytic Quarterly* 50:319–344.

Stern, D. (1977). *The First Relationship: Infant and Mother.* Cambridge, MA: Harvard University Press.

―――― (1983). The early development of schemas of self, other and "self with other." In *Reflections on Self Psychology,* ed. J. Lichtenberg and S. Kaplan, pp. 49–84. Hillsdale, NJ: Analytic Press.

―――― (1985). *The Interpersonal World of the Infant.* New York: Basic Books.

Stewart, H. (1977). Problems of management in the analysis of a hallucinating hysteric. *International Journal of Psycho-Analysis* 58:67–76.

―――― (1987). Varieties of transference interpretation: an object-relations view. *International Journal of Psycho-Analysis* 68:197–205.

―――― (1990). Interpretation and other agents for psychic change. *International Journal of Psycho-Analysis* 17:61–69.

Symington, N. (1983). The analyst's act of freedom as agent of therapeutic change. *International Review of Psycho-Analysis* 10:283–291.

Tansey, M., and Burke, W. (1989). *Understanding Countertransference: From Projective Identification to Empathy.* Hillsdale, NJ: Analytic Press.

Trevarthan, C. (1979). Communication and cooperation in early infancy: a description of primary intersubjectivity. In *Before Speech,* ed. M. Bellowa. Cambridge, England: Cambridge University Press.

Tustin, F. (1972). *Autism and Childhood Psychosis.* London: Hogarth.

―――― (1980). Autistic objects. *International Review of Psycho-Analysis* 7:27–40.

―――― (1981). *Autistic States in Children.* Boston, MA: Routledge and Kegan Paul.

―――― (1984). Autistic shapes. *International Review of Psycho-Analysis* 11:279–290.

―――― (1986). *Autistic Barriers in Neurotic Patients.* New Haven, CT: Yale University Press, 1987.

_____ (1990). *The Protective Shell in Children and Adults.* London: Karnac.

Viderman, S. (1974). Interpretation in the analytic space. *International Review of Psycho-Analysis* 1:467–480.

_____ (1979). The analytic space: meaning and problems. *Psychoanalytic Quarterly* 48:257–291.

Volkan, V. (1976). *Primitive Internalized Object Relations.* New York: International Universities Press.

Wangh, M. (1962). The "evocation of a proxy": a psychological maneuver, its use as a defense, its purposes and genesis. *Psychoanalytic Study of the Child* 17:451–472. New York: International Universities Press.

Winnicott, D. W. (1945). Primitive emotional development. In *Through Paediatrics to Psycho-Analysis,* pp. 145–156. New York: Basic Books, 1975.

_____ (1947). Hate in the countertransference. In *Through Paediatrics to Psycho-Analysis,* pp. 194–203. New York: Basic Books, 1975.

_____ (1949). Birth memories, birth trauma and anxiety. In *Through Paediatrics to Psycho-Analysis,* pp. 174–193. New York: Basic Books, 1975.

_____ (1951). Transitional objects and transitional phenomena. In *Playing and Reality,* pp. 1–25. New York: Basic Books, 1971.

_____ (1952). Psychoses and child care. In *Through Paediatrics to Psycho-Analysis,* pp. 219–228. New York: Basic Books, 1975.

_____ (1954). The depressive position in normal development. In *Through Paediatrics to Psycho-Analysis,* pp. 262–277. New York: Basic Books, 1975.

_____ (1956). Primary maternal preoccupation. In *Through Paediatrics to Psycho-Analysis,* pp. 300–305. New York: Basic Books, 1975.

_____ (1958a). The capacity to be alone. In *The Maturational Processes and the Facilitating Environment,* pp. 29–36. New York: International Universities Press, 1965.

_____ (1958b). Psycho-analysis and the sense of guilt. In *The Maturational Processes and the Facilitating Environment,* pp. 15–28. New York: International Universities Press, 1965.

_____ (1960a). The theory of the parent-infant relationship. In *The*

Maturational Processes and the Facilitating Environment, pp. 37–55. New York: International Universities Press, 1965.

_____ (1960b). Ego distortion in terms of true and false self. In *The Maturational Processes and the Facilitating Environment,* pp. 140–152. New York: International Universities Press, 1965.

_____ (1962). Ego integration in child development. In *The Maturational Processes and the Facilitating Environment,* pp. 56–63. New York: International Universities Press, 1965.

_____ (1963). Communicating and not communicating leading to a study of certain opposites. In *The Maturational Processes and the Facilitating Environment,* pp. 179–192. New York: International Universities Press, 1965.

_____ (1967). Mirror role of mother and family in child development. In *Playing and Reality,* pp. 111–118. New York: Basic Books, 1971.

_____ (1968). The use of an object and relating through cross identifications. In *Playing and Reality,* pp. 86–94. New York: Basic Books, 1971.

_____ (1971a). *Playing and Reality.* New York: Basic Books.

_____ (1971b). The place where we live. In *Playing and Reality,* pp. 104–110. New York: Basic Books.

_____ (1971c). Creativity and its origins. In *Playing and Reality,* pp. 65–85. New York: Basic Books.

Index

Sensation matrix
  isolation and, 173–176
  primitive isolation and,
    177–178, 179
Sexuality
  instinct theory, 195–196
  object relations and, 201–202
Sleep, isolation and, 177n
Spence, D., 15, 214
Splitting
  of consciousness, location of
    subject and, 13
  Kleinian psychoanalysis
    paranoid-schizoid position,
      dialectics, 35
    projective identification, 43
    subject integration dialectic
      and, 39–42, 48
Spruiell, V., 25, 215
Stern, D., 15, 171n, 172, 193,
  215
Stevens, W., 107
Stewart, H., 109, 215
Stimulus barrier, isolation and,
  168
Stolorow, R., 63n, 203
Structuralism, instinct theory
  and, 196
Structural model
  Das Ich/ego, 26
  Freudian psychoanalysis,
    consciousness/
    unconsciousness dialectic
    and, 20, 40
  Kleinian psychoanalysis,
    positions, dialectical
    interplay of psychic
    organizations, 38

Subject
  Das Ich and, 13
  Das Ich/ego, 26–27
  dialectic process and, 14
  Freudian psychoanalysis
    language of the subject, 25
    location in, 27–28
  Kleinian psychoanalysis,
    integration dialectic and,
    39–42
  Lacanian psychology, 28, 30
  object and, interdependence
    of, 62
Subjectivity. *See also* I-ness
  analytic third and, 5
  autistic-contiguous position,
    141
  consciousness/
    unconsciousness
    dialectic, 83
  depressive position, 143
  Freudian psychoanalysis,
    language of the subject,
    25
  Kleinian psychoanalysis, 33
    positional perspective, 35
    projective identification, 45
  projective identification and,
    8, 99–100
  Winnicottian psychoanalysis
    at-one-ness/separateness,
      50
    creative destruction of
      object dialectic, 56,
      58–59
    I-me dialectic of mirroring
      relationship, 53
    isolation and, 170